WOMEN'S PLACE

WOMAN'S PLACE

OPTIONS AND
LIMITS IN
PROFESSIONAL
CAREERS

CYNTHIA
FUCHS
EPSTEIN

University of California Press • 1970 •
Berkeley and Los Angeles

To my parents and to
Henriette R. Klein, M.D.

Creators of options

CONTENTS

LIST OF TABLES

ACKNOWLEDGMENTS

THOSE who are owed acknowledgments for providing the stimuli, the education, and the means which culminated in the writing of this book are many. Some were involved in its immediate preparation, some played a part far distant in time and were unaware of the active role they played as invisible but ever-present and scrutinizing guides. Although this work is a modest one, my debts are great and I shall take this opportunity to express my gratitude.

William J. Goode and Robert K. Merton not only provided the guiding sociological perspective but were inspiring mentors in the process through which the thinking of this book evolved. Professor Goode's directive to "get the book done" changed the context of endeavor from what seemed a herculean task to the workaday effort of the journeyman sociologist, a definition I never fully bought but which brought its dimension into realistic focus. Amitai Etzioni's general encouragement and suggestions were intertwined in the kind of motivating package which came just at the right moments.

Heinz Eulau, in provocatively introducing me to the behavioral sciences at Antioch College, is due a special quality of gratitude which this preface gives me opportunity to express. His insistence on excellence and his demonstration of analytic virtuosity which excited the imagination of all his students created a continuing quest for opening intellectual doors on the part of all who were exposed to his teaching.

If all women were exposed to the kind of intellectual excitement and pressures to aim high that these men offer to their students, this book need not have been written.

Howard M. Epstein also played a critical role in the life of the book. A true advocate of the equality of women, he helped refine many of the issues in the book and unstintingly applied his editorial talents in an attempt to improve the manuscript. His further attempts to reduce the role conflicts facing the working woman are acknowledged with gratitude.

The initial research for the project which resulted in the writing of this book was supported by a grant from the Institute of Life Insurance. A predoctoral fellowship from the National Institutes of Health and a grant from the Manpower Division of the Department of Labor provided the further necessary support for the completion of the project on women in the professions which is reported in this volume, and for continuing research in this same field.

I am obliged to a number of able assistants, Sheila Gallup, Rip Wilson, and Thomas Sykes, who helped at various stages of the research, and to the staff of the Bureau of Applied Social Research at Columbia University, notably its Administrator, Phyllis Sheridan, and her assistant, Madeline Simonson. Mrs. Muriel Bennett also saw to the typing of the final manuscript with her usual efficiency and good humor. I am grateful for the conscientious help of Jesse I. Fuchs (whose close association has been of value long in time) in proofreading the manuscript.

I also wish to thank the women who comprise my collegial network and who are my friends. They have brought that special kind of educated understanding of the dimensions of the processes outlined in this book.

Finally, my debt is acknowledged to Alexander M. Epstein, my most spirited educator in the dynamics of role-allocation.

You can see that we have started weeding the fields down there. The women work well. In the old days they weren't worth anything. Women were oppressed then, and people used to say: "An incompetent man can get about in nine countries, but a competent woman can only get round her cooking stove." When we began making our revolution, thirty years ago, the emancipation of women was one of the main points in our programme. We sang songs about it. I can still remember them. We had a slogan: "Free their feet!" Now their feet are free and women can work in the fields, so now, both men and women share in cultivating the land. Thirty years ago we were saying: "Let both men and women take part in our revolution," and now that has come about. Marriage is free now, too. It's only those directly concerned who have any say in it. That's a good thing. Women are hard workers. Do you see the women down there have baskets beside them as they weed, but the men don't? That's because the women aren't only weeding, they are also collecting grass for the family's pig.

Li Yiu-hua, Secretary of the Liu Ling People's Commune, Shensi, China, as told to Jan Myrdal in *Report from a Chinese Village.*

INTRODUCTION

IN the revolution of rising expectations — the struggle for the right to a chance to succeed — decades of silence have been broken by trumpet calls heralding the cause of women. The calls have been few, and most are soft rather than strident; they have given notice of women's hopes for full membership in American society but they have not yet succeeded in rallying mass support. There is more drama and more urgency in the plight of other groups, whose place at the bottom of society has resulted in potentially destructive social tensions. Women's place in society and in the home may have limited their horizons but it has not generated fears for the stability of society.

Furthermore, the public retorts, *women are free.* They are not downtrodden. They face no formal or legal barriers to any place in society. If they do not hold positions of responsibility and prestige, it is because they do not want them and have chosen to stay out of competition for them. Prestige and honor happen to occur in those domains which are typically male. Although women have pressed for admission to these spheres, once admitted they have expressed a clear preference for their own domain — the home. The home is their first concern, loyalty, and interest — and it is, they agree, their place.

There is a paradox in all this. Although women's place is said to be in the home, never before has it been seen as being so exclusively in the home, a view which is in direct conflict with the fact that the women of the underprivileged classes work today, as they have always worked. Women today constitute one-third of the labor force in the United States and in most industrialized nations. But that one-third is primarily made up of poor women who, not surprisingly, are working in jobs accorded the least prestige in our society. The problems of poor women are part and parcel of the general problem of poverty, one of the key concerns of our era, but they affect all women, including the prosperous and the highly educated.

Women's talents are underutilized and often repressed by our society, irrespective of social class. Even when women of high education and social class work, they, like the less educated and poor, tend to find that their place is at the lower end of the occupational range. Men from the elite classes become professionals or managers. But no matter what sphere of work women are hired for or select, like sediment in a wine bottle they seem to settle to the bottom. The tiny minority of women in occupations of high regard and reward — in the professions, for example — are generally found at their lowest levels. Although an overwhelming percentage of American women college graduates have gone to work in recent years (82 per cent of women graduates aged 20 to 24 were working in 1965), more than one-fifth of all employed women graduates were employed that year as service workers (including domestic work), factory workers, and sales or clerical workers.[1]

It has been charged that American society pays a high price for "keeping women down,"[2] yet it cannot be shown that a conspiracy or a grand design exists to keep them down. More important, there seems to be little awareness that they are not permitted to rise in society as individuals. Why women typically do not fulfill their promise — especially when that prom-

---

[1] U.S. Department of Labor, Women's Bureau, "Fact Sheet on Women in Professional and Technical Positions." Washington, D.C., November 1966, p. 4.

[2] Caroline Bird's, *Born Female: Or the High Cost of Keeping Women Down* (New York: David McKay Co., 1968), is devoted to this subject.

ise has been made explicit by liberal tradition and education—remains a question unanswered and rarely even asked.

Few middle-class women put the playthings of childhood behind them to assume the honored and rewarded occupational tasks of society. Their babies take the place of their dolls; their homes are substitutes for the dollhouses of yesterday. Those few women who wish to assume the tasks of adulthood and the challenge of the professional marketplace face difficult problems both at home and in the outside world. The gatekeepers of that outside world view them with suspicion, hostility, and amusement, even when they come to it with credentials that qualify them for admission.

In spite of these barriers to their full development, women do not typically feel that society has dealt with them unfairly, nor are they regarded by society as a particularly disadvantaged group. Their battles for legal equality have been won. They vote equally with men; they hold and trade property; they have access to educational opportunities. Only a few, although their numbers have increased, seem to be concerned with what they regard as the waste of women's talents and with dissatisfactions stemming from years of nonproductive activity after their children are grown. Most of these are regarded as malcontents and nonconformists.

Although similar in many ways to the discrimination faced by members of racial and ethnic minorities, the inequity faced by women in the occupations has its unique side. Women are inexorably seen in relation to their child-bearing functions and child-rearing tasks, the delegation of family roles to them, and men's historical dominance in the family and in society. The attitudes connected with the child-bearing function are those most commonly evoked in the discussion of women and work. These are often used as rationalization and justification for the status quo. What is, is regarded as necessary, natural, and just, and the effort to seek alternative solutions is thereby undermined.

Women in American society have not tended to view work

as central to their lives, as an avenue for self-expression and stimulation. In the lower economic strata, like men they work to support themselves and to augment the family income. Unlike men, who typically aspire to better jobs or more interesting work, they dream of not working, of joining America's gentry . . . middle-class women. Most middle-class women have viewed the occupational market as irrelevant, and work as supplementary and contingent. Their education is not supposed to provide them with more than enough general literacy to make them good mothers and companions — their principal right as members of the affluent society. Thus, from those women whose education could more fruitfully be directed toward careers in the wider world, few heroines have emerged. Our best women — those in whom society has invested most heavily — underperform, underachieve, and underproduce. We waste them and they waste themselves.

Why this is so and how it occurs is the focus of this book. The sociologist's special tools of analysis will be used to identify the social factors that assign women to their place and keep them in their place, and also arouse debate over whether this relegation is any longer necessary or desirable.

Women's lack of participation in the prestigious occupational spheres traditionally the reserves of men should be a matter of concern, for women, for society in general, and for the institutions responsible for educating women. Perhaps a change in women's position must affect all of society in some way. To the extent that her position is to be taken as a matter of "concern," this will be a value-oriented inquiry, based on the premise that it is good to better the condition of all individuals in society. The best should be models for the rest. Mothers can evoke visions of a better life for their sons and daughters if they have a vision of a better life for themselves. Women who view themselves as doers rather than takers may in time become less resigned to their plight and see the world as less overpowering. It is unfortunate today that poor and black working women are viewed as emasculating their men and improperly taking leadership of their families. Aside from the false assumptions on which these views rest (the women lead only by default and quickly defer once the man reappears in his traditional role), the notion that women who work are undermining the male, rather than sharing with him or operating equally with him, is a Victorian holdover.

The middle-class family pattern has been posed as a general model, and thus it has seemed unnecessary for society to seek innovative ways to solve the family problems of the poor. This family model in reality, however, is probably more representative of the upper part of the middle class. It is composed of a male breadwinner who works at a professional or managerial job and makes enough money to maintain an above-average standard of living. His wife may work but need not. The women of this middle-class stratum constitute a "leisure class," and devote themselves without pay to good works and tending to the arts and other cultural activities. Parents and children of such families are college educated and have tastes and manners which indicate their exposure to money and education, and their affiliation with others of their social position. Even more than their ability to assure their children's education, it is their not working that makes these women a symbol of affluence for the poor and aspiring lower class.

Unless social systems are indeed zero-sum situations in which one group may ascend only at the expense of another, it should be clear that raising the level of skill and productivity of poor women will add to the raising of the skill level and the aspirations of the entire system of impoverished people and may encourage, not subvert, the participation of the men. But if even the best educated and most socially nurtured women cannot succeed, how can poor women?

Similar sets of forces, often the same forces, are responsible for the selective occupational recruitment of women and for the underutilization of other groups and social categories that have not typically been defined as appropriate by the guardians of these elite places.

Problems of Participation

American women's participation in the prestige professions has remained constant during the past seventy years, increasing slightly since 1960 though not enough to constitute a change of level. This static situation has persisted in spite of astounding advances in the legal and social position of women in the United States and throughout the world. Women who have chosen careers in the elite professions are as deviant (in comparison with most American women) in 1968 as they were in 1898, although the notion of a woman doctor or lawyer is not as bizarre today as it was then.

Yet American women have not as a group clamored for more extensive rights and privileges. The daughters of the suffragettes have not attempted to build on the achievements of their mothers. The hard-won laws guaranteeing freedom of opportunity have never been fully implemented nor have women taken advantage of them.

Although the number of women in the labor force is enormous — some 28,000,000 and still increasing — women who work have settled for a fraction of the job possibilities offered by the economy. And their failure to advance into the jobs which are valued most highly in our society — the upper strata of business and the professions — is striking. Only a handful have joined the professions of law, medicine, teaching in higher education, engineering, or those linked to the natural sciences as Table 1 shows. The ministry and the military are the most enduring male preserves, and the proportion of women in them is negligible. A recent survey by the *Harvard Business Review* states that there are so few women in management positions that "there is scarcely anything to study."[3]

It is true that as our population grows a greater number of

[3] Cited in U.S. Department of Labor, Women's Bureau, "Fact Sheet on Changing Patterns of Women's Lives." Washington, D.C., March 1967.

TABLE I

Women in Selected Professional Occupations; United States

(percentage of all workers)

Occupation	1900	1910	1920	1930	1940	1950	1960
Lawyers	—	1.0	1.4	2.1	2.4	3.5	3.5
College presidents, professors, instructors	—	19.0	30.0	32.0	27.0	23.0	19.0
Clergy	4.4	1.0	2.6	4.3	2.2	8.5	5.8
Doctors	—	6.0	5.0	4.0	4.6	6.1	6.8
Engineers	—	—	—	—	0.3	1.2	0.8
Dentists	—	3.1	3.2	1.8	1.5	2.7	2.1
Scientists	—	—	—	—	—	11.4	9.9
Biologists	—	—	—	—	—	27.0	28.0
Chemists	—	—	—	—	—	10.0	8.6
Mathematicians	—	—	—	—	—	38.0	26.4
Physicists	—	—	—	—	—	6.5	4.2
Nurses	94.0	93.0	96.0	98.0	98.0	98.0	97.0
Social workers	—	52.0	62.0	68.0	67.0	66.0	57.0
Librarians	—	79.0	88.0	91.0	89.0	89.0	85.0

Sources: U.S. Bureau of the Census, *Census of Population*, 1960, Vol. I, Table 202, pp. 528–533. 1900–1950 statistics from U.S. Dept. of Labor, *Changes in Women's Occupations*, 1940–50, Women's Bureau Bulletin No. 253, 1954. p. 57.

TABLE 2

Women in Selected Professions

(Percentage of Total Personnel and Rate of Decrease or Increase of Each Sex)

(U.S., 1950 and 1960)

Occupation	Percent Female		Percent Increase or Decrease		
	1950	1960	Total	Female	Male
Lawyers and judges	3.5	3.5	16.9	18.5	16.9
Professional (total)	—	—	47.0	41.1	50.8
Biologists	28	27	51.2	38.2	56.6
Chemists	10	9	11.8	−3.6	13.5
Geologists, geophysicists	6	2	75.0	−27.3	81.1
Mathematicians	38	26	345.1	209.8	428.1
Physicists	6	4	87.8	20.2	92.5
All natural scientists	11	9	27.7	10.4	30.0
All engineers	1.2	0.8		11.0	64.3
Architects	—	—	27.8	−18.4	29.7
College presidents, professors, instructors	23	19	42.2	34.0	44.7
Dentists	—	2.1	10.1	−5.9	10.6
Engineers, technical	—	—	63.6	11.0	64.3
Physicians and surgeons	6.1	6.7	18.9	32.0	18.1
Social scientists	—	—	60.1	24.2	77.2

Source: U.S. Census of Population, 1960 Summary, *Detailed Characteristics*, PC (1) I D U S.

women are to be found each year in these elite occupational spheres, but in many expanding fields the rates of increase for women have been much lower than those for men. (See Table 2.) A sharp decline in the percentage of doctorates awarded to women in the physical and biological sciences is especially notable [4] and conceivably could foreshadow a further decline in female participation in these fields. The indication is, of course, that American women's participation in the professions has not had an especially progressive evolution.

Only a small percentage of professional women become part of the American professional elite or rise to positions of eminence. The United States has two women senators out of one hundred and, at last count, ten women representatives out of 435. Before her death in 1968, Lurleen Wallace was the only female governor in the United States, but it was common knowledge to Alabama voters that she was a figurehead for her husband, George Wallace, who could not, under state law, run for a third term. There have been only two other women governors in the history of the United States, both first elected in 1924: Mrs. Nellie Tayloe Ross of Wyoming and Mrs. Miriam Ferguson of Texas (who was reelected in 1932). Only two women have held cabinet rank in the federal government, and only six have served as ambassadors or ministers. Women hold a fourth of all jobs in the federal civil service but only 2 percent of the top positions.[5]

Few women are at the top anywhere in the world. Even with the Soviet Union's wide base of female professional personnel, the number of women decreases disproportionately as one goes toward the top in the Soviet hierarchy, both professional and governmental, and things don't seem to be getting better. *Pravda*, the Soviet Communist Party newspaper, not too long

[4] Lundsay R. Harmon and Herbert Soldz, "Doctorate Production in U.S. Universities, 1920–1962." National Research Council Publication 1142, Washington, D.C.: Academy of Sciences, 1963.
[5] U.S. Civil Service Commission Statistics Section, *Study of Employment of Women in the Federal Government: 1967*. Washington, D.C.: U.S. Government Printing Office, June 1968, p. 3.

ago deplored the fact that the percentage of women in leading positions in Soviet economic and political life was decreasing instead of getting larger. It was apparent that even Communist Party branches were reluctant to elect women to leading posts.[6]

This reluctance is true even in the so-called "feminine occupations." In library science, where women "man" the profession, a very large proportion of staff positions but only a very small proportion of administrative positions are held by women. Although women traditionally have made up a large part of the professional teaching corps, in 1964 only 22 percent of the faculty and professional staff in institutions of higher learning were women, a considerably smaller proportion than in 1940 (28 percent) and 1930 (27 percent). There has also been a sharp drop in the proportion of women secondary school teachers, 46 percent of the total in 1965 as compared with 57 percent in 1950.[7] The decline in percentage of women elementary school principals is almost extraordinary. In 1928, 55 percent of the principals were women; in 1948, 41 percent; in 1958, 38 percent, and in 1968 the figure has been reported to have dropped to 22 percent. In social work, another traditionally female field, there are a disproportionate number of male executives compared to the number of women working in the profession.[8]

Even granting that the top is available only to the few outstanding members of society, there are still millions of jobs available which are considered important and prestigious. Women don't do well with these jobs either, and in many instances their position has progressively deteriorated. Women held only 38 percent of all professional and technical positions in October 1966 as compared with 45 percent in 1940, reflecting a steady decrease in that period.[9]

[6] Reported in *New York Times* (August 25, 1965), p. 14.
[7] "Fact Sheet on Women in Professional and Technical Positions," *op. cit.*, p. 3.
[8] *Social Work Handbook* (New York: American Association of Social Work, 1950).
[9] "Fact Sheet on Women in Professional and Technical Positions," *op. cit.*, p. 1.

The pattern demonstrated by American women — being seen and not heard in the power centers of politics and the economy — is true as well for women in other societies, although the proportion of women who do work and who hold important jobs varies from country to country as Table 3 shows. While the proportion remains small in most countries, women's representation in professional occupations in Sweden, Great Britain, France, the Soviet Union, and Israel has doubled or more in the past twenty years. American women have not duplicated this achievement. Although the greater utilization of women in the economies of the Communist-bloc countries came about according to a plan, and because of huge wartime losses of manpower, other circumstances in the United States should have resulted in many more women seizing new opportunities. These circumstances are ideological and structural, and some of them are expressions of worldwide changes. They should have brought about far greater changes than those which did occur.

THE IDEOLOGY OF EQUALITY

Virtually the entire world has been swept by the ideology of equality for all. The inclusion of women in national economic life has not only been a necessity in many technologically advancing countries, but it is an expression of the emancipation of women everywhere from second-class citizenship. No doubt men and women have been granted the right to equality, in general terms, as a vague human right. However, for women the translation of that ideal into practice has been imperfect and unenthusiastic. Despite this comparative failure, the ideology has had considerable effect in giving women confidence in their right to select an occupation and the life style associated with it.

LEGAL CHANGES

Radical legal changes in the direction of equality for women are now worldwide and are to be found even in the most tradition-bound societies. In the United States, the provisions of

TABLE 3

Women in Selected Professions, by Country

Country	Occupation (Percentage)							
	Lawyers	Physicians[a]	Dentists	(Judges)	Engineers[e]	Scientists	(Physicists)	(Chemists)
U.S.	3.5	6.5	2.1	2.0	1.2	7.0	5.0	7.0
U.S.S.R.	36.0	75.0	83.0	30.0–40.0	28.0	38.0[d]	—	—
U.K.	3.8[b]	16.0	6.9	[c]	.002	6.4	—	—
Japan	3.0	9.3	3.0	—	—	—	—	—
Sweden	6.1	15.4	24.4	6.7	1.3[f]	—	—	—
Germany (Fed. Rep.)	5.5	20.0	—	—	3.3	—	—	—
Germany (Dem. Rep.)	30.0	—	—	30.0	—	—	—	—
Italy	2.8	4.9	—	0.5	1.1[f]	—	8.1[h]	10.7
India	0.7	9.5	3.9	—	—	—	—	—
Denmark	—	16.4	70.0	—	—	—	—	—
Poland	18.8	36.4	77.0	—	8.0	—	—	—

Sources: U.S. figures from Margaret Mead and Frances Kaplan (eds.), *American Women* (New York: Charles Scribner Sons, 1965); Elizabeth Shelton, "Are the Scales Weighted Against Women Judges?" *Washington Post*, September 19, 1965; United States 1950 and 1960 censuses.

Soviet figures from L. Dubronina, *Soviet Women*, printed in U.S.S.R. (n.d.), Professor V. Elyutin, D.Sc., "Higher Education in the U.S.S.R.," London, 1962, Soviet Booklet No. 100; Norton Dodge, *Women in the Soviet Economy* (Baltimore: Johns Hopkins Press, 1966). United Kingdom figures from 1961 census, Summary tables, General Register Office (lawyers and judges, chemists, physical and biological scientists).

Japanese medical figures from American Medical Women's Association report of July 11, 1966.

Swedish figures from James Rössel, "Women in Sweden," The Swedish Institute, Stockholm, Sweden, p. 5: figures on basis of 1960 census. Note too that these percentages are reflections of small absolute numbers: the 6.1 percent for lawyers is for 80 out of a total of 1,530.

German (Federal and Democratic Republic) figures from Helmut Steiner, "Social Origin and Structural Pattern of the Body of Judges in the G.D.R.; Comparative Approach to the Corresponding Body in West Germany," Sociological study group at the Institute of Economics, German Academy of Sciences, Berlin (mimeographed), May 1966.

Italian figures from 1961 Italian Census from Instituto Centrale di Statistica, Direzione Generale dei Servizi Tecnici, May 19, 1967.

Indian figures from 1961 Indian Census, Vol. I, part 11B(u), General Economic Tables, Table B-V.

Danish figures from 1960 census.

Polish figures from Magdalena Sokolowska, "Some Reflections on Different Attitudes of Men and Women Towards Work," *International Labor Review*, 92 (1965), pp. 35–50.

[a] Other countries (excluding the Soviet bloc) with large percentages of women doctors are the Philippines (24.7), Finland (24.2), and Israel (24.0). Women make up between 7 and 12 percent of the physicians in Brazil, Canada, Norway, the Netherlands, France, and Australia. Source: American Medical Women's Association, 1740 Broadway, New York City. (Report of July 11, 1966.)

[b] The figure is only for barristers. Source: *Time*, August 27, 1965.

[c] Only one woman Queen's Counsel has become a judge in 400 British courts. *Ibid.*

[d] Includes "scientific personnel, higher educational institution teachers, heads of research institutions" (120,200). 1959 figures from Dodge, *op. cit.*, p. 299 (94,000 reported by the U.S.S.R. Central Statistical Administration, March 12, 1958, presented in *Facts on File*, March 13–19, 1958).

[e] Additional (I.L.O.) figures cited in M. Alexandrova, "Position of Working Women in Capitalist Countries," *Daily Review* (translations from the Soviet Press, Pushkin Square), Vol. IX, No. 157 (2411), July 2, 1963. Canada has 24 women engineers out of a total of 17,700; Australia 6 out of 12,000; Italy 220 out of 28,200.

[f] Includes architects.

[g] Includes mathematicians, astronomers, geologists.

Title VII of the Civil Rights Act of 1964 further reduce legal inequalities in the sphere of employment. Official guidelines to Title VII provide that employers will no longer be permitted not to hire or promote women on the ground that their fellow workers or customers would not accept them; to classify certain jobs exclusively for males or females unless sex is a bona fide qualification; to establish separate seniority lists based on sex; to label jobs "light" or "heavy" when they are merely a subterfuge for the terms "male" or "female"; to forbid the hiring of married women if the ruling is not also applied to married men; to place newspaper help-wanted advertisements excluding applicants of one sex and limiting the job to applicants of the other sex.[10]

In Japan, radical legal changes in the status of women was insured by the new constitution of November 3, 1946, which guaranteed equality under the law to all Japanese, stating in Article 14: "All people are equal under the law and there shall be no discrimination in political, economic or social relations because of race, creed, sex, social status or family origin." According to this article, all Japanese women are to be treated without discrimination from men in all phases of life — political, economic, and social.[11]

World-wide, the United Nations *Newsletter on the Status of Women* reported that as of March, 1968, women may vote in all election and be eligible for election in 117 countries; only seven countries still prohibit voting rights for women[12] and four others impose limitations.[13] In 1967 the General Assembly of the United Nations unanimously adopted a "Declaration on the Elimination of Discrimination Against Women" which

[10] House Resolution 7152, *Congressional Record* 110 (May 25, 1964), p. 11847.
[11] Takashi Koyama, *The Changing Social Position of Women in Japan* (Paris: UNESCO, 1961), p. 16.
[12] Jordan, Kuwait, Liechtenstein, Nigeria (Northern Region), Saudi Arabia, Switzerland (except cantons of Basle, Geneva, Neuchatel, and Vaud), and Yemen.
[13] Congo (Democratic Republic of), Portugal, San Marino, and Syria.

guarantees (at least in principle) a broad range of rights to equality in education, work, marriage.

INDUSTRIALIZATION AND PROFESSIONALIZATION

Women have worked in all societies. In the West, industrialization removed the site of work from the home but created new occupations and a rising demand for personnel at all levels, much of it recruited from the female population. In most of the Western world, including the United States, women constitute between a third and a half of the labor force; typically they are clustered at the lower levels of administrative work rather than in production, and in the para- or sub-professions rather than in the high-ranking professions. Between 1940 and 1967, the number of employed women in the United States more than doubled, rising from 13,840,000 (25 percent of the total working force) [14] to 28,000,000, and women's share of jobs continues to increase. Women were 37 percent of all workers in 1968, numbering 28,700,000.[15] By 1970, it is expected to reach 30,000,000 out of 86,000,000 jobs. The trend may stop, however, or even reverse. William J. Goode notes that, in some Western countries, women's participation in the labor force has remained somewhat stable and in a few cases has proportionately decreased.[16] However, they remain underrepresented in positions of responsibility and those requiring creativity and talent.

HIGHER EDUCATION AND PROFESSIONAL TRAINING

Women have gained access to higher education and professional training in many countries. Doubtless they will achieve it universally in time. But although discrimination still exists in this area, the actual opportunities for professional training are seldom exploited to their fullest by women. (Their participa-

[14] U.S. Department of Labor, Women's Bureau, *1962 Handbook of Woman Workers*, Bulletin 285 (Washington, D.C., 1963), p. 4.
[15] U.S. Department of Labor, Wage and Labor Standards Administration, "Background Facts on Women Workers in the United States," September 1968, p. 1.
[16] William J. Goode, *World Revolution and Family Patterns*, p. 61.

tion in education will be examined more fully in Chapter III.) In view of these new educational and professional opportunities, why do women continually settle for the lower-ranking, lower-paying, and often unchallenging work of their society? This is particularly true of the United States. Yet, how may we explain that some women — those who make up the female 3 percent of the legal profession and the female 8 percent of the medical profession, for example — successfully deviate from the mainstream pattern of American women? What are the factors that influence women's decision to work, their choices of occupation, and their levels of aspiration? Which are the forces that once made the United States lead in the push for women's equality, and which are the forces that have directed American women away from the economically and intellectually rewarding work of society?

The fact that a stratum of educated, trained, and professionally active women exists at all makes it unnecessary to argue the question of women's innate intellectual capacities or their ability to do sustained, high-concentration work. The question of whether women are as intelligent as men, or whether they can handle abstract ideas and solve problems, has been eliminated by their achievements in even such male-dominated fields as mathematics, chemistry, physics, law, and the social sciences. It is clear that, as with any other segment of society, not all women possess the intellectual capacities for professional or other upper-level work, and that even if all occupational barriers were removed not all of those who possess such qualities would aspire to careers. The question that arises is even so why have so few capable women ever fulfill the promise of their potential and ability; and, conversely, how do those few who do, manage it?

We know that not all talented men succeed in their occupations, and that demonstrated ability in science, engineering, and the law may not inevitably bring a man success. But, unlike women, capable men generally expect to do well and, if they do not, like Job they may feel justified in questioning the justice of the universe. Men expect financial reward and satisfaction from their work and can look to their families and peers for approval and support of their efforts.

But the woman who has proved her capabilities in training generally cannot count on society for encouragement or her colleagues for fair treatment. She faces a difficult decision in weighing whether to begin on a career that almost inevitably will involve her in a conflict with traditional images of her place in society and, perhaps, with her own images of personal fulfillment. Once past the initial barriers, she may be forced repeatedly to review her decision as she faces successive conflicts between her personal life and her career. She will also have to decide whether to aim for the rewards men would expect as a matter of course: money, prestige, power, and work satisfaction.

Whatever her decisions, it is likely that she will have to compromise far earlier and for far less than the man. Whatever her decisions, it will be extraordinary if her intelligence and application bring equal rewards from a society that has promised her nothing less than equality.

I

IDEALS, IMAGES, AND IDEOLOGY OF WOMEN AND WOMEN'S ROLES IN AMERICAN SOCIETY

THE problems faced by professional women in their work and personal lives cannot be investigated meaningfully without examining the cultural themes and the value system that bear on the roles of women in American society. These social images and values form a fundamental part of the context in which women's decisions about careers are made. They coexist — or conflict — with occupational images and values which help to define some kinds of work as appropriate or inappropriate for women, and thus figure both in the selection of a profession and in the recruitment patterns of the professions.

The culture of a society provides the framework within which its members must operate and the standards to which they must conform. Though cultures are always changing, most behavior patterns show considerable continuity, and successive generations often exhibit strikingly similar beliefs and attitudes. This is true especially of beliefs which are of a general character, as they are likely to be in a society's images of what is manly and what is womanly.

Values, ideology, and images form much of the context in which the socialization processes shape occupational and family life. From their culture, children derive a set of expectations about themselves that become a crucial part of their self-image. From the value system, they learn what to like and dislike, what to cherish and disdain, and, central to the purpose of this study, what are acceptable occupational and family-social patterns. They are taught to define certain work as essential and of high value and other work as essential but of low value. Depending on their social class, race, and sex, specific types of work are encouraged, tolerated, or tabooed. This early conditioning is nearly always crucial to later occupational decisions.

Yet American culture, like other cultures, encompasses many values and social images which are often incompatible and contradictory.[1] It is no surprise to any observer of American life that the image of the perfect woman, the values and norms revolving about the female role, and the very participation of women in the professions are contradictory, ambiguous, and sources of personal strain. The primary source of this stress is ambivalence, conceptualized as sociological ambivalence. Merton and Barber see this as the social state in which a person, in any of his statuses (as wife, husband, or lawyer, for example), faces contradictory normative expectations of attitudes, beliefs, and behavior which specify how any of these statuses should be defined.[2] Each of the contradictory expectations is often as le-

---

[1] Robert Lynd enumerates many of these popular beliefs in a discussion of contradictory assumptions in American life in *Knowledge for What: The Place of Social Science in American Culture* (New York: Grove Press, 1964), chapter 3.

[2] Robert K. Merton and Elinor Barber, "Sociological Ambivalence," in Edward A. Tiryakian (ed.), *Sociological Theory, Values and Sociocultural Change*, pp. 91–120. "Sociological ambivalence" subsumes a number of structural ambiguities also labeled by Erving Goffman as "affiliative cross-pressures," "claims of a multi-situated kind," "identification with one type of

gitimate as the next. This ambivalence, rooted in the social structure and not a product of any individual's personality problems, can severely undermine training, aspiration, motivation, and planning and make difficult the definition of future roles.

For the girl, ambivalence and ambiguity arise from the contradictions posed by images of the female role, occupational and professional roles, and American society's values of equality and achievement. The stresses stemming from this complex of role- and value-conflicts are major factors in the career development process of women, particularly at the points of initial decision, entry, and measurement of success. These cultural and structural processes create conditions which act to limit women's participation in prestige occupations and alter their capacity to fulfill professional norms.

The Image of the Female Role

All societies define sex roles according to their images of the ideal man or woman. It cannot be too radical to assert that no human being is unaffected by these definitions, or can escape being measured according to these cultural images.

Although preferred female attributes and behavior vary over a considerable range,[3] in most societies there is a core of preferred and imputed feminine attributes. In American society these include, among others, personal warmth and empathy, sensitivity and emotionalism, grace, charm, compliance, dependence, and deference.

Leopold Rosenmayr traces the current feminine-role image from European literature and the arts, which glorify the woman as desirable and beautiful and to be won only if the male fulfills certain requirements of socio-economic status.[4] After

---

structure at the expense of another," and "heterogeneous commitments and attachments," in *Encounters*.

[3] Margaret Mead, *Sex and Temperament in Three Primitive Societies*, is, of course, the classic reference.

[4] Leopold Rosenmayr, "The Austrian Woman," *International Social Science Journal* 14, No. 1 (1962), 157–65.

becoming a wife — a basic component of the female role — the woman becomes the center of the home, crowned with the virtue of faithfulness and responsible for harmonious coordination of house and family. Consider the current female models of American society — Jacqueline Kennedy recently was rated first in a Gallup poll of "most admired women," [5] followed by Mrs. Lyndon Johnson; both were "admired" as attractive women, interested in art, beauty, and fashion and devoted primarily to their families. Eleanor Roosevelt, a doer and a mover, aroused a good deal of public hostility, and there was considerable social comment, in her day, about the inappropriateness of her activity. Despite the fact that woman worked outside the home even in the Middle Ages, and was and is a working partner in peasant societies, her desired attributes, according to Rosenmayr, were the ones glorified by the urban middle- or upper-class role-ideals, in which the expectation of what the woman should be and do was linked with the man's desire for beauty and pleasure and his demand for order and relaxation after work. [6]

Preferred female attributes and behavior vary universally over a considerable range. Margaret Mead has dramatically illustrated this by pointing to disparate patterns in some preliterate societies, [7] and in more advanced societies as well we find that qualities defined as male in one society may be defined as female in another. Edward Hall writes: "In Iran . . . men are expected to show their emotions. . . . If they don't Iranians suspect they are lacking a vital human trait and are not dependable. Iranian men read poetry; they are sensitive and have well-developed intuition and in many cases are not expected to be too logical. . . . Women, on the other hand, are considered to be coldly practical." [8]

Women's talents have been acknowledged, too, but are chan-

[5] N.Y. *World Journal Tribune* (December 28, 1966), p. 16.
[6] Rosenmayr, *op. cit.*
[7] Mead, *op. cit.*
[8] Edward T. Hall, *The Silent Language*, p. 10.

neled by social definition. As Negroes have been said to "have rhythm" and have made their mark in the jazz world but not in commerce, so women are said to "have intuition" and a gift for handling interpersonal relations and are encouraged to become social workers. Yet, men who work well with people are defined as "good diplomats" and are given important political-executive posts which are closed to women and their imputed skills. Women are assumed to be emotional, in the sense of not having the capacity to control or channel their emotions in productive ways. For example, a recent study of employment practices showed that women were denied advancement, especially to executive positions, because employers felt that they were "too emotional," though the writer observed that no employer objected to the man who might "blow his stack." [9] The perceptive though slightly facetious characterization of the feminine image offered by Morton M. Hunt, author of a popular book about the complexity of women's roles, is also commonly held: "The female is, and was meant forever to be, warm, nurturant, yielding, lovable though a bit on the stupid side, willing to accept the rule and domination of the male, a bit fractious but much improved by being beaten once in a while." [10]

The image of woman includes as well some noncharacteristics: lack of aggressiveness, lack of personal involvement and egotism, lack of persistence (unless it be for the benefit of a family member), and lack of ambitious drive. In fact, the spectrum of behavioral traits, like passivity, aggressiveness, practicality, and so on, found in all members of the human species have become sexualized and are assumed, asserted, or expected to correlate with sexual differences. [11]

Conflict faces the would-be career woman, for the core of at-

[9] Charles Ginder, "The Factor of Sex in Office Employment," *Office Executive* (February, 1961), p. 10.

[10] Hunt, "The Direction of Feminine Evolution," in Farber and Wilson (eds.), *The Potential of Women*, p. 260.

[11] The consequences for women's productivity in the arts is noted by Barbara Herrnstein Smith, "Masculinity and Feminity in the Arts," speech at Bennington College, Bennington, Vermont, April 19, 1968 (mimeographed).

tributes found in most professional and occupational roles is considered to be masculine: persistence and drive, personal dedication, aggressiveness, emotional detachment, and a kind of sexless matter-of-factness equated with intellectual performance.

Since the female and professional role-configurations are painted by this society as mutually exclusive rather than overlapping or concurrent, most American women feel they must choose between them. Those who attempt to combine them must deal with many strains. The problem is further complicated; the womanly virtues are not all that is expected of American woman. Although her image is centered on the domestic role, the American woman, nevertheless, has been viewed as competent and able — as were pioneer women — and at times has been expected to work competently outside the home. There were thousands of Rosie the Riveters in the United States (in Europe as well) during World War II, though American women are not expected to be mechanically inclined. A recent French study of women in the metals industry indicated that employers felt women were incapable of doing work requiring a mechanical sense — those who demonstrated they were capable were termed "exceptions" and "phenomenons." [12]

Women who work in male-dominated occupations in particular are often thought to be sexless. The woman who takes her work seriously — the career woman — traditionally has been viewed as the antithesis of the feminine woman. This was especially true of women who chose to work in the traditional male professions before World War I. It was an image accepted by women themselves. Women reinforced the image by wearing mannish attire and often choosing to remain single. Many accepted the notion that the traits required of a professional woman and those required of a feminine woman were mutually exclusive. Women who did attempt to demonstrate both

[12] Madeleine Guilbert, *Les Fonctions des femmes dans l'industrie* (Paris: Mouton & Cie., 1966), p. 135.

sets of traits — and their numbers have increased substantially in recent decades — risked surprising or confusing their role-partners. The colleagues, friends, and others with whom they came in contact often did not know how to react to them; should one, for example, assume an easy familiarity with or a protective distance from one's female co-worker?

Another type of ambivalence arises because men and women may perform the same activities and have the same aspirations irrespective of the expectations normally linked to their sex statuses. There is no perfect matching of occupational and sex roles. If female and male sex-role components were clearly exclusive, and clearly linked to certain jobs (only men, and no women, could be lawyers, for example), perhaps the consequences would be less troublesome or dramatic for the person who wished to take a job seldom selected by his or her sex. If the injunction against a woman ever exhibiting assertive or ambitious behavior was total, and, if the stress on female compliance, charm, and nurturance was matched by the requirement that women remain at home, there would be no alternatives open, no career decisions to be made, and a minimum of role conflict to endure. Women would know and stay in their place.

Combinations of Sex Roles and Professional Roles

Female role models which incorporate the attributes of independence, objectivity, and assertiveness and thereby violate society's common image of femininity repel many men and women. Helen Hacker's study of working women documents the ambivalence and disapproval facing the woman who displays "male" virtues: "Negative feeling may attach to her for being ambitious for herself directly or in furthering her own interests to the detriment of her family. Thus, while 'ambitious' is a positive attribute for men, there is some question if a woman is complimented when she is called ambitious." [13]

[13] Helen Hacker, "A Functional Approach to the Gainful Employment of Married Women," unpublished Ph.D. dissertation, Columbia University, 1961, introduction, p. 5.

Not only must the woman not possess characteristics considered male attributes, she must bear the added burden of women s generally low evaluations of themselves. Hacker identifies this as minority-group self-hatred, stemming from the subordinate group's acceptance of stereotyped concepts of itself held by the dominant group. Women everywhere refer to female "cattiness" and disloyalty. They claim to dislike other women, assert they prefer to work for men, and profess to find female gatherings repugnant. This set of attitudes constitutes a barrier to women's aiming high in the occupational world. For those who do aim high we suspect there is some difference in the self-image they hold, or that they consider themselves exceptions to the general view they have of women's capacities and potential. My own study of women lawyers[14] did not attempt to measure self-evaluations, but it was clear that the women lawyers interviewed rated themselves highly and felt that others in their profession thought highly of them. This seemed to indicate that professional esteem can flourish only where women are protected from the low evaluations of other women.

There has been some change in these attitudes but it is hard to tell just how much. In 1946, a *Fortune* poll[15] showed that women even more than men had misgivings about women's participation in industry, the professions, and civic life. From observation and discussion with women in and out of professional life, I believe it is clear that women continue to have mixed feelings about those of their sex who challenge male prerogatives.

Negative or ambivalent feelings toward women in areas of work defined as demanding or requiring assertive characteristics were demonstrated by findings of the 1961 College Graduate Study of the National Opinion Research Center.[16] When women college graduates were asked why they thought few

---

[14] "Women and Professional Careers: The Case of the Woman Lawyer," unpublished Ph.D. dissertation, Columbia University, 1968.

[15] *Fortune* (September 1946), p. 5.

[16] Reported by Alice S. Rossi, "Barriers to the Career Choice of Engineering,

American women enter medicine, engineering, or the sciences, many pointed to the negative images men have of women who enter these fields — particularly engineering. Fifty-six percent of the sample felt that men in engineering resented woman colleagues, and 61 percent said that women were afraid they would be considered unfeminine if they entered the field.[17]

Women who select the domestic life often resent and deride those of their sex who choose careers, in the same way that lower-class Negroes who have acquired dominant-group attitudes toward the Negro often have resented upper-class Negro pretensions to superiority.[18] Domesticated women also feel the career woman is neglecting the duties of "her proper station." Hacker has reported that working women often accept the common definitions of their place and share with the housewife a negative view of the working wife.

The working wife, no less than the housewife, says that the working wife is nervous, ambitious, well-educated, selfish, and up-to-date. She further concurs with the housewife that the working wife is not a loving mother, a good wife, nor efficient in household tasks. True, she is not as emphatic as the housewife in deeming the working wife nervous and selfish, and she is more prone to claim the virtues of wife and mother, but the direction of feeling is similar for both groups of wives.[19]

The pattern of self-hatred or group disparagement is not untypical among women professionals. From my interviews with women lawyers [20] I had the impression that, although they respected themselves, they often had negative things to say about other women lawyers and did not care to be identified with "women lawyers" as a social category. Many observed that

Medicine or Science Among American Women," in Mattfield and Van Aken (eds.), *Women and the Scientific Professions*, p. 95.
[17] *Ibid.*
[18] This comparison has been offered by Helen Hacker, "Women as a Minority Group," *Social Forces* 30 (October 1951), p. 66.
[19] Hacker, dissertation, *op. cit.*, chapter 2, p. 26.
[20] "Women and Professional Careers," *op. cit.*

other women attorneys worked "to compensate for their failure as mothers and wifes." One lawyer who had retired from active practice felt that women lawyers tended to be failures as women. When asked if she had women-lawyer friends, she observed: "No, but I know a lot although I don't often see them. I just occasionally run across them. I found that the ones who have unhappy marriages were the ones who pursued their careers; . . . the ones who had happier marriages, were the ones who did as I did, which was to pursue a rather inactive variety."

Another lawyer, married and in active practice, felt that other women in her field also tended to have personality disturbances: "I must say that the women I've met in my profession — most of them — I don't know whether it's because most of them are not happy people — have had crack-ups of various kinds. That is, those who have stayed with it [law]. A number have very aggressive personalities. I find them interesting. But I'm not sure their careers have done them any good in their personal development. They are not feminine women."

The husbands of several of these women, encountered when their wives were interviewed, similarly observed that women lawyers were aggressive or hard to deal with, always excluding their wives from the characterization.

Women in other professions are also commonly viewed as difficult people by these men.

The Pattern of Revocability

The absence of positive, supportive images relevant to the working woman's life results in the possibility that she can stop her advance in a career or abandon it altogether at almost any time. At every turning the American woman is faced with a fresh decision of whether or not to work. And at each point of decision strong norms exist which weigh against going on.

The married, middle-class woman who works does not live a day without the knowledge that she can choose not to work and that, on balance, a decision to give up working probably will meet with more social support and approval than any arrangement she may have worked out to harmonize her work and home life.

Lotte Bailyn has commented that "Occupation: Housewife" is an ever-present alternative. The constant possibility of revocability makes the modern working woman's problem more complicated than the either-or choice earlier feminists faced.[21]

Models and Images

Until recently the traditional images of the ideal female role have not been challenged by competing images, even where women have abandoned traditional roles by seeking and attaining professional rank. As a result, both women and men continue to accept traditional images though women's behavior does not conform to them.

Bruno Bettelheim has pointed to society's selective inattention and ambivalence toward women who work:

The little girl's first storybooks and primers, for example, hardly ever show a woman as working or active outside the home. It makes no difference that over five million American children under twelve have full-time working mothers. The little girl is expected to shape herself in the image of the maternal housekeeping women in these stories, and never mind what certain unfortunate mothers may be obliged to do. And emphasizing society's ambivalence, the image of the stay-at-home woman is presented by her female teacher, who may well be a working mother. In these early years, it is rare indeed for girls to hear the slightest suggestion that they might one day do the interesting work of this world quite as well as many men, or even better.[22]

[21] Bailyn, "Notes on the Role of Choice in the Psychology of Professional Women," *Daedalus* 93 (Spring 1964), 707. Goode cites opinion polls in a number of Western countries to support this contention, although many of his data are drawn from working-class population. William J. Goode, *World Revolution and Family Patterns*, pp. 54–66.

[22] Bruno Bettelheim, "Growing Up Female," *Harper's* (October 1962), p. 121.

Before the recent public debate over modern women's complex roles, models different from the traditional were rare and encountered only by chance. The low percentage of women in professional life was probably at least partially a reflection of the fact that those who ultimately chose a profession did so idiosyncratically, rather than through a sequence of introduction, training, and assumption of career. Women in our law study professed only vague memories or no memory at all of why they had chosen law as a career; few had known women lawyers and, although some knew men lawyers, there was no reason to assume that the masculine pattern could be followed by a girl. One eminent woman lawyer who was interviewed remembered that her brothers were expected to join her father in his successful law practice; but such a goal was not set for her. Until chance led her to question her father, she remarked, "I didn't think much about being a lawyer while I was gowing up, but I remember the first time that I had any recollection of even thinking about it. I was walking along with Father, and a little bit of a thing, and it's kind of a hop and a skip to keep up with his stride, and all of a sudden there came out of me, and it must have surprised me as much as it did him, this little thing said, 'Can girls be lawyers, Father?' And Father looked down and smiled at me and said, 'Why not, my dear?'" In this case, the challenge met a positive response and an image was molded for the girl. This happens to few girls, however. Even today there are virtually no stories, movies, or plays which have as a theme the happy, fulfilled career of a woman to whom work is part of a normal life.

In modern societies, the favored norms and images are channeled and transmitted by the popular media as well as by the traditional channels of personal influence and exposure. Films, televisions, and popular magazines stress the romance which leads to marriage and then children. Betty Friedan's survey of ten years of fiction in popular women's magazines [23] finds that

[23] "The Happy Housewife Heroine," chapter 2 of *The Feminine Mystique*, pp. 33–68.

the working women in the stories are usually pictured as frustrated and unhappy until they find the "right man" and retire to homemaking. Today's *Cosmopolitan* magazine has broadened its perspective and actually is slanted toward the career-girl audience, although the emphasis is still on glamour and how to catch a man. To some extent, *Mademoiselle* magazine, with a heavy college-age readership, is giving young women some exposure to women "doers" in a broad array of occupations.

It is unusual to see popular fiction which has as its central character the happy career woman, married or single by choice, whether artist or opera star, much less lawyer or surgeon. Here clearly truth is stranger or more accurate than fiction, for real cases of fulfilled productive women can be found though they are conspicuous by their absence in storyland. There have been a few novels about women in the professions which have been based on the lives of real women but they have not been widely read. I do not know of any major author who has written about women of this type.

A young girl may learn of or have contact with a woman who has freely chosen to subordinate marriage to her work, but she will hardly hear of her through the movies or television. The single working woman past her early twenties is likely to be portrayed in the popular media as embittered, frustrated, forsaken, displacing her real desires for marriage and children to a career — though she may appear as the home-wrecker who infects the world of the virtuous and happy homemaker and whose only hope is for rehabilitation in her own home with her own children. The women of action in television plays are usually young single women or divorcees. One rarely, if ever, encounters a story in which a married career woman goes off to work leaving her children in the care of a housekeeper or baby-sitter, or even a fond grandmother. Of course, storyland models are not all-powerful — young men grow up to marry even though Superman and Batman have remained bachelors through the years. But perhaps the reason the little girl doesn't aspire to become Lois Lane is that she believes it would be necessary to have Superman at her side in order to be an effective female newspaper reporter.

Even the popular and professional conceptions of the mental health of the American woman stress the performance of the female in her traditional statuses as mother and wife. Both Friedan and Rossi [24] have observed that in the post-World War II period, the conservatism of both psychology and sociology seriously undermined any attempt to expand the feminine role. Rossi has observed:

Sociologists studying the family borrowed heavily from selective findings in social anthropology and from psychoanalytic theory and have pronounced sex to be a universally necessary basis for role differentiation in the family. By extension, in the larger society women are seen as predominantly fulfilling nurturant, expressive functions and men the instrumental, active functions. When this viewpoint is applied to American society, intellectually aggressive women or tender expressive men are seen as deviants showing signs of "role conflict," "role confusion," or neurotic disturbance.[25]

The attitudes of social scientists have lent considerable legitimation to the popular suspicion that women who seek an independent identity outside the home are women with problems and that women who don't feel a strong drive to establish a family first and foremost should wonder what is wrong with them. Many women who in recent years sought the solution to their discontent on the analyst's couch often heard their own worst fears corroborated and were persuaded to try to cast their lives more contentedly in the feminine (read "domestic") mold. It is not uncommon to hear the vocabulary of psychoanalysis used popularly to put women "in their place." Women in male occupations or with male-typed aspirations fall prey to the label

[24] Alice S. Rossi, "Women in Science: Why So Few?" *Science* (May 28, 1965), pp. 1196–1202; and Friedan, *op. cit.*

[25] Alice S. Rossi, "Equality Between the Sexes: An Immodest Proposal," *Daedalus*, Spring 1964, p. 611.

of "castrating women" or hear accusations that they are not feminine. The accusation is usually powerful and debilitating to the woman.

Given these popular images and cultural definitions, it well may be a sign of mental disorganization if a woman chooses to reject the primacy of the domestic role; in any event, she is surely a deviant case by the standard of what is normal in her society.

Of course, the popular images and values mesh in public taste. Even those who might admit woman's right to push for achievement or excellence find that they don't care for the woman who does so. If the American girl dreams of a strong man who will make his mark in the world yet protect her, the American man dreams of a girl about whom he may feel protective — someone soft and yielding. This is so although many men have a psychological need not to take care of but be cared for; the strong and dominant woman has no place in the American dream.

Not Either/Or, but Both

Women who choose careers react to the cultural expectations of feminity by trying to prove themselves in all spheres. They accept all the role expectations attached to their female status, feeling that to lack any is to deny that they are feminine. This is as true in 1968 as it was in 1890. Robert Smuts recounts the story of a well-to-do and active New York woman, a Mrs. Maude Nathan, who accepted the entire definition of being "a good wife." Mrs. Nathan

lived in a fashionable New York brownstone, with a staff of four servants, during the 1880's and 1890's. When she began to work with women's organizations on behalf of social reform, her husband's family was disturbed. Her autobiography tells how she sought to allay their misgivings and prove her womanliness by devoting herself diligently to household duties. She did all the marketing, purchased materials for and planned and supervised the home manufacture of linens, underwear, and her own dresses and hats, closely supervised the servants, and once a year, put up a year's supply of pickles, preserves, and corned beef.[26]

Mrs. Nathan's story is not unlike that of one prosperous New York attorney (whose annual gross income averaged $50,000), who told me she shopped daily for groceries, after arising at 6:00 A.M. to do the housecleaning before her nursemaid appeared to care for the children. Other successful professional women in America today are prey to the idea that they must attend to the drudgery of the household in addition to their occupational duties, not for the sake of economy but because they do not feel comfortable about delegating household tasks to others. Clearly only women with extraordinary vigor can attempt to fill all these expectations.

The Cultural Theme of Equality

Women are said to be the equals of men in American society[27] and entitled to share in the nation's riches and opportunity. The interplay of these values with the images and ranking attached to the female role is complex and raises many questions. What, for example, is the effect on women of the core values of equality and achievement in American society? Although many sociologists have pointed out that various American groups and subgroups hold to the society's values differentially,[28] these values remain valid on the whole. These are, of course, general values, without strict definition; we suppose that they are commonly linked to "success," as measured by economic gain, and are taken to mean that there are equal

[26] Robert W. Smuts, *Women and Work in America* (New York: Columbia University Press, 1959), p. 15.

[27] "Equality in this sense does not mean equality in condition, but rather universalistic treatment in all sectors." From footnote in Seymour Martin Lipset, *The First New Nation*, p. 229.

[28] Herbert H. Hyman, "The Values Systems of Different Classes: A Social Psychological Contribution to the Analysis of Stratification," in Reinhard Bendix and Seymour Martin Lipset (eds.), *Class, Status and Power* (New York: Free Press of Glencoe, 1953), pp. 426–442.

chances to attain success. There is no doubt that women share these values with men, as a result of exposure to their social stratum, age, or ethnic group allegiances.

The ideology of equality further specifies that all should fully exploit their potentials and that the exploitation of an individual's potential is beneficial to society. It implies conversely, that society loses when it fails to utilize talent. It remains clear, however, that specific talents are attributed to particular social categories — that they are socially defined and associated with a class, a sex, or an ethnic group, thus setting the major theme of equality against some assumed and underlying themes of inequality.

The issue of women's rights raises an important example of the clash of equality values. Few would argue any longer against full legal rights for women, but many still cannot adjust to the participation of women in public and professional life on an equal basis. Poet Eve Merriam succinctly characterized the popular attitude in her comment, to a meeting of the Harvard Club of New York City, that "sex prejudice is the only prejudice now considered socially acceptable."[29]

It has been shocking to me to find that even members of the radical Left in America, among them participants in the Spring 1968 university student uprisings at Columbia University, express traditionally conservative views about women's rights to equal employment opportunities and equal pay for equal work. One professed Marxist asserted in as conservative a manner as any businessman: "Women don't need the money as much as men who have families to support." (During the student takeover of Columbia campus buildings, a call went out for women volunteers to cook for the hungry strikers. One young female revolutionary protested that "women are not fighting the revolution to stay in the kitchen," and the call was amended to ask for *people* to man the kitchen.)

The revolutionary Left has been challenged from the inside for its conservative attitude toward women, for its "conde-

<hr />

[29] "What Educated Women Want," *Newsweek* (June 13, 1966), p. 71.

scending" approach to women's problems, and for its under-utilization of women's talent in decision-making positions. The *National Guardian*, a leftist New York weekly newspaper, noted the paucity of women in top posts at the 1968 Conference of the New Left,[30] and the publication of a new group called New York Radical Women attacked a *Ramparts* magazine article on the Women's Liberation Front[31] for applauding the use of passive rebellion as an appropriate women's weapon against the "establishment."

The inequalities women face in the occupations and in politics was certainly not the subject of an important plank in the platform of any of the political parties in the 1968 presidential campaign. Doubtless these problems are not regarded as issues, and the cause of women is not linked to the general thrust for civil rights. In fact, in its push for equality, the black movement — the Black Muslims in particular — has pushed for a more traditional middle-class role for Negro women, urging that they be kept in the home and relieved of their economic role. The participation of black women in the occupational sphere has been pointed to as a disruptive element in the Negro family and as a contributor to the emasculation of black men. Most Negro women who work do so out of economic necessity; the problems faced by the black community lie not in the fact that the women work but that opportunities are closed to the men. Were the men to have open opportunities, the fact that their women worked should not affect their self-images. Certainly no one has suggested that the pattern of many middle-class professional Negro families, where both spouses work and where the families are intact, might be a positive model for the white middle class to emulate, though it is one of the closest models to equality between the sexes we have in American society.

Thus, there has been a move toward matching the black sex-

[30] Susan Sutheim, "Women Shake Up SDS Session," *National Guardian*, June 22, 1968.
[31] Lynn Piartney, "A Letter to the Editor of *Ramparts*," *Notes from the First Year*, June 1968.

stratification structure to the white, but with few people concerned with achieving true equality of the sexes in any group. The notion of equality, of course, is ambiguous enough to be interpreted broadly and comes into conflict with many norms linked to other spheres. For example, family norms which prescribe a ranking hierarchy in which wives defer to husbands in major decisions are not expected to vanish in the face of equality. Although Americans deplore the Japanese custom of wives following their husbands by a few paces, they feel it is appropriate for their own wives to stand silently aside when they are discussing "important issues" with other men. Women are supposed to enjoy deferring to men and to consider it an accomplishment to know their place; it is a component of feminine charm. There is some evidence that women defer to their male children as well as to their husbands and fathers, thus teaching their girl children early who is considered of most value. It is unseemly for a girl to be a tomboy, but to use the term "sissy" to a boy is a far more violent attack upon him.

Sexual Equality Not Social Equality

There have been some radical changes in the images of certain aspects of the female role, especially as concerns the woman's right to sexual fulfillment — that is, the orgasm — equally with the man. Few social scientists [32] have been alert to the fact that women have felt freer to speak up about their rights in the sexual sphere than in the social sphere. And these rights have been granted, more and more. In fact, women have been conceded privileges which guarantee freedom in sex relations. On campuses, for example, there is certainly strong feeling and a movement toward granting women the same curfew hours and residence options as the men. College women have access to "the pill" and information about other contraceptive devices. Consider the storm of protest which resulted when a co-ed was

[32] Jessie Bernard is one exception. See her "The Status of Women in Modern Patterns of Culture," *Annals of the American Academy of Political and Social Science* 375 (January 1968), 13.

threatened with dismissal from Barnard College because she was found to be living in an apartment off campus with her boyfriend. Even the sedate *New York Times* carried front-page stories about the controversy. The ACLU considered handling her case; the Protestant minister and the rabbi of Columbia (admittedly liberal men) expressed their support of the girl, and the Barnard Judicial Committee reviewed her case and recommended that she not be suspended.

Public opinion has indeed changed since the days in which women merely endured the embraces of husbands who regarded female sexuality as a characteristic only of wanton women. As Professor Ira Reiss has demonstrated in the report of his national survey of premarital sex attitudes and behavior, although it is not true that more students are "doing it" than before, more of them approve of sexual intercourse before marriage, and we can expect a behavioral change in the direction of keeping attitudes and action congruent.[33]

Sexual Equality Not Status Equality

Sexual equality has not been achieved coterminously with sex-status equality, however. The right of women to the equal practice of sexuality is largely established and is discussed openly and without embarrassment among the educated and probably soon throughout American society. Respectable national women's magazines such as the *Ladies' Home Journal* and *McCall's* carry articles almost every month dealing with some aspect of sex in detailed clarity.[34] Yet sex-status equality is still a slightly distasteful issue, often masked by irrelevant humor. Even women in elite positions in American society ac-

---

[33] Ira L. Reiss, *Social Context of Premarital Sexual Permissiveness.*

[34] J. P. Greenhill, "Sex and Pregnancy," *Redbook* (April 1965), pp. 28 *ff.*; S. Frank, "The Most Delicate Problem in Marriage," *Good Housekeeping*, March 1967), pp. 87 *ff.*; S. Milas, "Why I Believe in Sex Before Marriage," *Redbook* (October 1967), pp. 139–142; H. Ginott, "Husbandese: The New Language of Intimate Persuasion Between Husband and Wife," *Ladies Home Journal* (February 1968), pp. 61 *ff.*; and a monthly column in the *Ladies Home Journal* edited by D. C. Disney entitled "Can This Marriage Be Saved?" which discusses the sexual problems in marriage and techniques for solving them.

cept the cultural censure on the topic and reject association with spokesmen for the sex-equality cause. These women, as well as those in the most liberal colleges and universities, typically will fight for civil rights for Negroes but shun the fight for civil rights for women. Although the women's suffrage movement was linked to the abolition movement, the civil rights movement today has only minimally attempted to further the quest for women's opportunity in the right to achieve. The introduction of sex into the provisions of the 1964 Civil Rights Act was an attempt to impede its passage, although, of course, its consequences, unanticipated as they were, helped women to fight employment discrimination. There are some civil rights advocates who have supported the attempt to achieve women's equality, but these are few and too great a proportion of them are considered to be eccentrics.

Sexual Neo-Traditionalism

Interestingly enough, the reaction to the achievements of equality in the sexual sphere is neo-traditionalistic — offered by both sober and sensation-seeking sociologists and their popularizing brothers. Equalization has been confused with desexualization. Jessie Bernard, who certainly encourages women's opportunities, nevertheless wonders "how much equality can the sexes stand," worrying that the psychological costs may be too high for men.[35] Vance Packard worries that, because of a 10 percent rise in premarital sexual intercourse among college students since the 1940's, the moral code and sex-role differentiation are crumbling; and Charles Winick sees the increasing popularity of king-size beds and other aspects of the material culture as indices of the domination of an ambiguously androgynous concept of sex-role detrimental to individual identity and the useful organization of society.[36]

[35] Bernard, *op. cit.,* p. 14.
[36] Packard, *The Sexual Wilderness: The Contemporary Upheaval in Male-Female Relationships.* Winick, *The New People: Desexualization in American Life.*

Alice Rossi's suggestion [37] that a more androgynous view of the sex division of labor might be stimulating and beneficial to members of both sexes (girls would be permitted to play with trains and speak their mind and boys would learn that it was good to be tender as well as tough) has not been popular with either social scientists or laymen.

Since the achievement of female suffrage, women's rights movements have suffered in numbers, support, and power. The Lucy Stone League and the National Woman's Party, for example, are considered by many to be crank organizations and have little success in winning young members. The National Organization for Women (NOW) has had more success, given by the current interest in the waste of women's talents and the leadership of Betty Friedan, whose book, *The Feminine Mystique*,[38] aroused interest throughout the world. NOW has had some political successes (broader implementation of Title VII of the Civil Rights Code of 1964, for example) [39] but it still suffers from the stigma attached to its cause and the fact that its membership tends to be drawn from among unmarried women. In addition, a small number of radical women in New York City, some of whom call themselves the "Redstockings," linked to various dissident groups on the college campuses (Columbia University in particular), are hoping to mobilize women in the colleges in the push for equality. As of April 1969, their numbers were few although they attracted a hundred women to a first meeting to discuss issues and tactics. Probably their activity was an index of wider interest in the problems of women than has been demonstrated in recent times, but it is too early to sense whether or not their effort will be aborted early in conception or will gather momentum. As this volume went to press I attended the first Congress to Unite

[37] Rossi, "Equality Between the Sexes," *op. cit.*
[38] New York: Norton, 1963.
[39] A notable recent achievement of NOW's efforts was the ruling of the Equal Employment Opportunity Commission that it was illegal for employers to fill most jobs through separate "male" and "female" help wanted advertisements. *New York Times* (August 6, 1968).

Women, a meeting in New York City of some 15 groups of women dedicated to "women's liberation," and attended by about 300 participants. About 80 percent of the women — men were excluded — seemed to be college students or graduates, under 30, single, interested in professional careers, and to the political left. Their proposed solutions to women's social problems almost always entailed radical changes in the social structure.

Are Women Separate But Equal?

Many critics of the push for women's participation in occupations and professions claim that although women's treatment reflects their obvious differences, they are honored equally with men in the society. However, this view conflicts with the American value of achievement, upon which we typically base honor in our society.

Achievement — establishing one's place in society by one's own accomplishments — is reinterpreted for women. Women are held to achieve through their husbands. Their status and prestige come primarily as a result of their husbands' accomplishments and rank in society. Only rarely is the woman's accomplishment in even purely female activities considered genuine success. The title "Mother of the Year" has less meaning in the United States than in the Soviet Union, where genuine approbation is given to the woman who bears many children. It is clear that if women are to achieve and be respected for their achievements, they must do so in the world of men — as measured by pecuniary success, power over the destinies of others, and the opinions of colleagues.

If women do not do the work rated highest by society, can they ever be valued in the same way as are men? The findings of a number of social scientists have indicated that there is a preference for male children rather than female children (especially as first-born).[40] Men are valued more and so people wish

---

[40] Among them are Margaret Mead (*Male and Female,* London: Victor Gollancz Ltd., 1950, p. 266); Robert R. Bell (*Marriage and Family Interaction,* Homewood, Ill.: The Dorsey Press, 1967, rev. ed., p. 261); and Amitai Etzioni, who makes note of several studies, including that of Charles F. Westoff, noted population expert ("The Social-Psychological Structure of Fertility," in *Inter-*

to have sons. There is evidence that man is on his way to developing biological science to the point where he can predetermine the sex of children. Husbands may one day decide the sex of their offspring by taking pills.[41] Should men decide to use this knowledge, there is good cause to worry that the world's sex ratio would become severely lopsided. We would then truly have a man's world in numbers as well as dominance.

So, even in equal America, our cultural preference is for boy babies. It seems to be a universal preference. We treat our girl babies well and love them and take care of them as they grow. But we never regard them as highly as we do boys. It is striking that in the societies where women are permitted to participate in honored work, such as Israel, they are also generally accorded more honor. The honor accorded "gentle womanhood" in American society has always had the consequence of assigning women to a sphere separate from men. The pedestal is never an equalizer, and woman on a pedestal is seen through eyes which alternate between adulation and condescension.

There are other ironic consequences of the strong current toward equality in America today. For example, alterations in the social structure have occurred which place additional impediments in the way of women who wish to pursue equality in work. The domestic labor traditionally performed by the lower-ranking members of American society — Negroes and immigrants — has been given a heavy negative valence because of the new movement toward equality. Young lower-class girls now prefer to work in offices and factories, shrinking the reservoir of surrogate care for children and the home. Because domestic labor is sex-typed as a female job,[42] the middle-class

---

national Population Conference, International Union for Scientific Study of Population, Vienna, 1959), which indicate that there is at least a 55 to 65 per cent greater demand for male children than for female children. Etzioni further suggests that when sex control becomes feasible an imbalance in favor of males is quite likely: Amitai Etzioni, "Sex Control, Science and Society," Science 161 (September 13, 1968), 1107–1112.

[41] This development was forecast by Professor Charles Birch, head of the Sydney (Australia) University School of Biological Sciences, on his return from the Twelfth International Congress on Genetics in Tokyo, Japan.

[42] Consider, too, that if this kind of sex-typing were altered, many employ-

housewife finds she must do it herself; low-ranking housework thus has become the major specialty of the educated women. Not only have such women not rebelled at their lot, but they often have enlarged the scope of domestic activities to include such things as gourmet cooking and home dry-cleaning. Appropriately, these activities have been redefined as suitable and even desirable for upper-middle-class women, and the woman of this stratum who delegates them to others feels as if she has failed to do her duty.

Thus, women may be encouraged to enter the professions and occupations, but they are expected to perform a delicate balancing of roles in which they will have little assistance from society's hierarchy of value-priorities. There is clearly a preference for the woman who exhibits what are defined as feminine characteristics, and often only lip-service will be paid to her other qualities. (It may be distasteful to argue a case against a woman attorney who uses feminine wiles rather than pleading her case as a man would, but the opposing attorney might be the first to point out that the straightforward-acting woman is not "feminine.") Men appear to want women to be feminine but are uncomfortable working with feminine women. A woman biochemist recently told me of her problem in finding an appointment in research. In spite of her more than adequate scientific credentials, part of the problem was that she was indeed quite "feminine." Had she been a plain or reserved person, she observed, she might have been classified as a "neuter," but she was not and several male scientists told her frankly that it would be unsettling to have her around.

Many men and women claim to believe in equality yet clearly prefer that the female role center on the home and being a helpmate. It is true that middle-class men generally tend to voice credos of equality for women, although we do not know how they would feel about real competition from their wives. William J. Goode suggests that middle-class men's opinions often

---

ment opportunities would become available to unskilled young men, who might find the relatively unstructured work of the household attractive.

are far more liberal than their actual behavior as measured by their demonstration of authority within the family.[43]

"Proper" Motivation for Careers

The conflict of values in American society again emerges when we raise the question of what women should work for. In Soviet society, social pressure is clear and positive in the direction of participation in the work force by all who are able. Women's work is considered good for the country, good for the woman, and good for the children.[44] In the United States, as in other Western societies, the woman may work for money if it is needed by the family; but she is considered selfish if she leaves her home during the day to work for her own enjoyment.[45] In the Soviet context, a woman would be expected to explain why she *is not* working; in the American setting, she has to explain why she *is* working. Eighty-four percent of a sample of American professional women, when asked why they worked, said it was an economic necessity.[46] And, of a sample of English mothers with jobs, the largest single group (44 percent) gave financial reasons for not staying home. Only 29 percent gave professional or vocational interests as their reason for working.[47]

Goode notes that women say they are motivated to work because they need the money, yet he shows that when professional women were asked if they would leave their work if economic pressure was lessened most said they would not.[48] It is likely that American women who wish to work because of job

[43] William J. Goode, *World Revolution and Family Patterns*, pp. 21, 67–70.
[44] David and Vera Mace, "The New Soviet Woman" in *The Soviet Family* (N.Y.: Doubleday, Dolphin Books Edition, 1964), chapter 5, pp. 92–116. See also H. Kent Geiger, *The Family in Soviet Russia* (Cambridge, Mass.: Harvard University Press, 1968).
[45] Hacker, dissertation, *op. cit.*, chapter 2, p. 26.
[46] Marguerite Zapoleon, "College Women and Employment," in Opal D. David (ed.), *The Education of Women*, p. 51.
[47] Simon Yudkin and Anthea Holme, *Working Mothers and Their Children*, p. 44.
[48] A sample of German women is given as an illustration. Goode, *World Revolution and Family Patterns*, op. cit., p. 65.

satisfaction often feel they must offer another, more acceptable reason: economic necessity. American women may further be internalizing their society's ascetic Protestant ethic, according to which one should work but enjoyment is not an appropriate work goal.

Consider the effect of "image" on the working patterns of women. The American image of working women is limited and negative. Work is not commonly considered a component of the status attributes of adult women. Yet one-third of the U.S. labor force is composed of women, most of them apparently not visible to society or its values. In contrast, the popular impression of Soviet society is that Soviet women do work. *New York Times* reporter Elena Whiteside, reporting on a visit to relatives in the Soviet Union a few years ago, recounted:

Out of close to twenty young and old women with whom I talked at length, not one was without a profession or was not studying for one. They included a Ph.D. and professor of ancient history about to retire; a 40-year-old unmarried editor of a regional newspaper; a vivacious, witty dental surgeon; a 20-year-old pharmaceutical student; a retired high school teacher; a retired economist in a hat factory; a 35-year-old engineer who builds bridges; a Ph.D. and M.D. doing research on tuberculosis in Moscow; a young mother of a boy of four who had married early and was now taking correspondence courses to become a teacher of Russian literature; a 25-year-old guide at the Historical Museum (the mother of a 4-year-old son, she had majored in French history at the University of Moscow); a 24-year-old surveyor from Leningrad; collective farm workers; a draftsman with the railroad in Moscow.[49]

This account gives the clear impression that for Russian women, work outside the home is a natural and ordinary activity. It is hardly descriptive of a representative sample, but other observers, including American social scientists,[50] have found

[49] Elena Whiteside, "For Soviet Women: A Thirteen-Hour Day," *New York Times Magazine* (November 17, 1963) pp. 28 ff.
[50] Participating at a conference on the Role and Status of Women in Soviet

Soviet women routinely working at a wide range of jobs, including those normally considered man's work in the United States (mining, bus driving, etc.).

TABLE 4

Women in the Work Force
(selected countries)

Country	Percent
Austria	40
Czechoslovakia	44.4
Rumania	45.3
West Germany	36.7
France (1963)	33.3
United States (1968)	37.0
Italy (1963)	28.8
Great Britain (1962)	34.4
Belgium (1963)	31.6
Luxemborg (1960)	26.6

Source: Phillip Shabecoff, "German Women in Jobs Increase," *New York Times,* March 21, 1965; "Women Comprise 40% of the Austrian Work Force," *New York Times,* February 18, 1965; *The French Woman: The Picture in the 1960's,* in *French Affairs,* No. 190A (April 1966) (New York: Ambassade de France, Service de la Presse et d'Information), p. 9.

Paradoxically, the fact is that women constitute 40 percent of the Soviet labor force — not greatly different from the American figure of 37 percent and exactly comparable to the situation in Austria, where 40 percent of the work force is made up of women (see Table 4). There may, of course, be some discrepancies in work-force definitions. Probably more Soviet women work at non-work-defined jobs than do American women — on farms, at full-time care of grandchildren, etc. But what is interesting is the image attached to work for the woman. Urie Bronfenbrenner reports that many Soviet women who are not

Russia, Bryn Mawr College, Bryn Mawr, Pa., April 23–25 1964 (Mark Field, Urie Bronfenbrenner, et al.).

working are studying in order to be able to work. A young Soviet woman economist recently in the United States told questioners that she had left her young child home in the care of her mother-in-law and husband while she spent a year abroad. She noted that *her* mother had a full-time job of her own and that the "babushka" — the classic helping-hand grandmother — more and more was dying out as an image as well as in reality. She said that *she* certainly would be occupied with her work at the time she expected to be a grandmother.

Social Definitions of Sex Roles

Social definitions are intrinsic to the individual's self-concepts, and help to shape hierarchies of choice, definitions of rewards, and pressures creating guilts. These have direct consequences for the sex-division of labor. If women are to work only if they have to, then they will not have the foresight to train or to orient their lives in the direction of work. They will drift to the easily accessible and unskilled jobs. That many occupations are considered "male" and others "female" has considerable effect on the early socialization process of the individual and on recruitment and performance later in life.

Though there is no society in which a substantial percentage of the work force is not made up of women, there are only a few which match the fact with cultural images and ideals which facilitate and foster women's work. Many societies have legislated reforms and provided a legal framework for equality of economic opportunity for women. But there is probably no modern society, with the exception of those of the Communist countries,[51] in which expectations of female-role behavior include a constellation keyed to women's participation in the productive and prestigious work of the economy. In the Soviet-bloc countries, a heavy infusion of ideology, coupled in some cases with dramatic shortages of manpower resulting from losses in World War II, created norms that encouraged women

[51] The ideology exists in Israel but it seems limited to the population of the kibbutzim.

to hold jobs and become part of the professional world. Ideology is an essential part of the equation. West Germany also lost a considerable proportion of its men (among those over 35, the surplus of women reaches about 4 million; and 1.8 million families lack a father) without striking changes in the composition of its professional labor force. Motivation, however, implies the promise of rewards and the hint of sanctions as well; Soviet woman is not only encouraged to work for the good of the economy, the polity, the society, and her own fulfillment, but her decision not to work often brings admonishments for economic parasitism, treason to the cause of equality of women, and reactionary and traditionalist spirit and behavior.

While in other lands the emancipation of woman was linked with her right to vote, in the Soviet Union it has been linked with her right to earn a living. Freedom from economic dependence on man was considered the true breaking of her age-old shackles. Women are not obliged to work, but those women who remain at home are referred to as "drones." [52] The recruitment of women into the Soviet economy should remain constant, if it does not increase, because it will remain normative for women to train and otherwise prepare to work. Whether or not they actually do work, particularly during the child-bearing and child-rearing years, remains conditional on the availability of surrogate care. It will be up to the Soviet society to assure this care; if it does not, a return to traditional patterns could result.

The Effect of Economic Values

Many obstacles to women's participation in the professions arise from American attitudes toward money and the use of capital. American society in many ways is more pragmatic than ideological, in the sense that economic gain is accepted as a better rationale for behavior than any other ideological value. In our society, waste is deplored and we are able to command atten-

[52] Mace and Mace, op. cit., pp. 23–24.

tion with the cry that women's talent is being wasted and that society must find ways to utilize their productivity;[53] we do not, however, admit that the problem is one of the individual's right to fulfillment.

Attitudes toward money and waste thus bear heavily on how the education and training of women are handled both on private and public levels. Here the public, or governmental, sector is probably far ahead of the private sector. There is an underlying value ascribed to calculated risk-taking for potential profit which makes woman's educational lot difficult. Education is considered an investment in the future, and even banks now give low-interest loans for college education because they believe that it will lead to higher income later, as has in fact been demonstrated. But where the potential payoff is considered too small to make the investment worthwhile, or where there is no sense that one is gambling on a good thing, Americans are cautious. In a traditional middle-class European household, a girl's education might be supported because of the family's concern that its children be "cultured." Americans want to know what practical advantage will result from a college education.

This attitude is independent of the fact that America does broadly educate its women as well as its men. Partly this is because, especially among the middle class, a B.A. or at least some college is considered essential to a girl's making a good marriage. Without college, she has less opportunity or bargaining power in the marriage market, and she certainly is excluded from the important channel of social mobility that a good marriage may provide. Further consequences of the "pragmatic-

[53] This is the burden of a number of articles and books published on the subject within the past ten years, among them Mary I. Bunting, "A Huge Waste: Educated Womanpower," *New York Times Magazine* (May 7, 1961); John B. Parrish, "Professional Womanpower as a National Resource," *Quarterly Review of Economics and Business* (February 1961); and Seymour M. Farber and Roger H. L. Wilson (eds.), *The Potential of Women* (New York: McGraw-Hill Paperbacks, 1963). Newer books are not as direct. Among them are Caroline Bird, *Born Female: Or the High Cost of Keeping Women Down* (New York: David McKay Co., 1968); Robert Staller, *Sex and Gender* (New York: Science House, 1968); and Edwin C. Lewis, *Developing Woman's Potential* (Ames, Iowa: Iowa State University Press, 1968).

orientation" of the American value system, particularly with respect to economic return, are discussed in Chapter III.

Circumventing Problems in the Value System

The American value system fails to provide cultural support for women who would become professionals, but it also possesses flexible characteristics which permit departure from dominant images and attitudes. These constitute a framework in which decisions favoring careers for women can be made.

First, values are usually posed so generally that they can be redefined and reinterpreted to provide a rationale for many disparate types of behavior. For example, although protection for women may be used to enforce humane treatment during pregnancy, it has also been used to exclude them from certain male-designated occupations. Women, however, might take advantage of the ambiguity to press for entry to some field or other and to seek advancement on it.

Second, under certain conditions individuals can more easily depart from norms. Many values apply differentially to different segments of the population. Upper-class women in the United States, for example, may have more freedom to deviate from the popular image of the proper housewife and to engage in political life, as their counterparts do in other countries.

Third, as institutions — and thus roles — change, the value system and normative structure change; transition periods cause ambivalence but also mean that new values are formed and many outmoded values and beliefs are discarded.

The value system and behavior are, then, interactive. In what follows we will explore some of the social processes affected by dominant values, those which are instrumental in changing values, and the conditions under which alternative sets of values are activated. The value system may create straight paths for some and dead ends for others. But most often the roads wind, and some happen upon the proper routes either by chance or because they have special directions.

II

THE SOCIALIZATION
PROCESS AND ITS
CONSEQUENCES: ROADS
TO CAREERS & DEAD ENDS

WHEN does the distinction between the occupational roles of women and men begin? It is the distinction which makes certain jobs male and others female, which narrows women's vision of which work may become theirs. Women learn early that most professional jobs are men's jobs and do not think about the possibility that a woman might decide to take one of them. If women exclude themselves from the competition for professional jobs, we cannot blame professional recruiters with discrimination. Discrimination is more complex than commonly supposed and acts to limit women's horizons much earlier in the life cycle than at the point of looking for a job. It begins in the cradle, where boys and girls begin receiving different messages about their future roles. This early socialization is important in establishing the identity of the individual, but we may question why the messages to girls about what they may become occupationally, is so much more confining than those sent to the boys, assigning girls the jobs toward the lower end of the prestige hierarchy. Because of their socialization, girls tend to accept the definitions of what they might do; they do not aspire high. Even the smart ones, those who could become quaified, never are motivated sufficiently to attain the skills they would need later to become members of the professions. Although middle-class girls have a better chance to get a college education than lower-class girls, they seldom go on to get the necessary additional training necessary for working at jobs at the professional level. The socialization of the typical American woman affects the motivation even of the college educated women and usually undercuts her career potential.

Early Socialization

It is generally assumed that the skills required in the sciences and professions can be acquired by all those who have a basic competence and who will apply themselves to the task of learning. Yet women of demonstrated scholarship do not plan or proceed with careers. Girls with good college records often are more satisfied with a job that will provide good chances to meet a potential spouse than with one that gives them an opportunity to gain professional training and experience.

Setting aside the problems of the job market and the reluctance of those in command in the professional and business world to invest in the training of those they consider probable career dropouts, we can see quite clearly that many of the career limitations on women are self-imposed. When it comes to jobs, women generally have minimal aspirations, choose short-run social and economic advantages, and fail to question the social definitions and expectations of their motivation and their capacities.

These self-limitations probably are initiated as early as infancy, when cooing relatives reinforce the dependency of the girl child while at the same time demonstrating approval of the aggressions of the boy. The boy is encouraged to reach out, to expand his capacities in running, climbing, and building; the girl is shielded and directed away from physical activity. At the outset of the impress of society's mold on the child, the girl is the recipient of a larger share of punishment for insubordination, aggression, ambition, and the other qualities that would lead her development beyond the world of the family. On the other hand, her brother's sights are directed to the vastness of the sea, to outer space; into his child's world are introduced symbols of strength, mobility, and power — the rocket ship, Superman, the towering crane, and racing cars.

Dependency Training

Even the egalitarian middle class in the United States, which gives boys and girls an almost identical formal education, rears its boys more permissively than its girls.[1] The boys are permitted to act out their aggressions, but girls are not supposed either to feel or to display aggression (though they are permitted to cry and boys are not). Respondents to a study of middle-class fathers by Aberle and Naegele admitted that "we know that some boys are holy terrors in their play groups," but none expressed any concern that their sons might be bullies and some proudly guessed that their boys were "a bit of a devil." Some of these same fathers were troubled by "bossy" daughters. The girls' desired behavior seemed to focus strongly on their being "nice," "sweet," pretty, affectionate, and well-liked.[2]

For girls, compliance and willingness to please are clearly valued traits. Girls also are held in tighter rein, making their activities more susceptible to observation and sanction. In a study of a few years ago, Mirra Komarovsky showed, in quantified detail, that, if one held income constant, girls went to college nearer home than boys and that to many families (and to the

[1] See Urie Bronfenbrenner, "Socialization and Social Class Through Time," in Eleanor Maccoby et al. (eds.), Readings in Social Psychology, pp. 400–425.
[2] David F. Aberle and Kasper D. Naegele, "Middle-Class Fathers' Occupational Role and Attitudes Toward Children," American Journal of Orthopsychiatry 22 (April 1952), pp. 366–378, cited from A. Inkeles (ed.), Readings on Modern Sociology, pp. 100–107.

girls themselves) their education probably was not thought to matter quite so much as that of the boys.[3]

We might infer that the women these girls become, once attuned to the opinions of parents and family, are sensitized generally to the opinions and preferences of others (other-directed, in the Riesman sense). It may be this very propensity which makes women more people-oriented than object-oriented,[4] and gives them the empathetic responsiveness that leads many of them into social welfare work. Whether this is an innate or an indoctrinated propensity, indeed whether or not women are in fact more compassionate, empathetic, and more interested in people than are men, is yet to be scientifically demonstrated. But there is no doubt that women are thought to be so[5] and this belief has manifold consequences for society's allocation of womanpower.

Role Models

The socialization that begins in infancy to mold women to cultural images continues through childhood and adolescence into adult life. One of the agencies of socialization is, of course, the presence of adequate role models, those who provide examples for a young person to follow. For a young boy to grow to manhood in the full cultural normative sense, ideally he must observe grown men performing their designated roles — conscientiously going to work, helping their children, being good husbands. We are aware of the unfortunate consequences arising in those sectors of American society where young boys cannot find in their fathers models of what the culture defines as ideal behavior, for example among Negro slum youths who do not see men of their group assuming permanent jobs, supporting their families, or aspiring to positions of responsibility.

In stable societies it is normal for boys and girls to learn their

---

[3] This work is reviewed in her book, *Women in the Modern World: Their Education and Their Dilemmas.*

[4] To use Herbert Gans's dichotomy; see *The Urban Villagers,* chapter 4.

[5] Following W. I. Thomas's observation that "If men define situations as real, they are real in their consequences," requoted, for example, in R. K. Merton, *Social Theory and Social Structure,* p. 421.

future roles by imitating their parents and other adult members of their community. The youngsters not only learn how to become farmers and doctors but they also learn to find these occupations attractive. Of course, if sheer imitation were continuous from generation to generation, societies would hardly change. But as conditions change in a society, so must roles change. Sometimes, as Inkeles found in studies of child-rearing in post-revolutionary Russia,[6] parents themselves become agents of change by educating their children for the life they believe will be typical in the new society. Young people more often take the initiative, rejecting their parents' world view as inappropriate for the times, and attempting to build a different kind of life for themselves. This is especially true where the parent generation is an immigrant group[7] and the generation gap is more radically obvious. Immigrant parents typically act as negative role-models; they represent the opposite of what the youth wants to become. Rejecting his parents as models, the youth may then search for alternative models. (Note that this rejection is different from the situation in which immigrant parents themselves direct their children to follow the new ways.) Where society is in a state of flux, alternative models may be military heroes, national political figures, or other idealized types, often emerging from the peer culture. It is important to distinguish, however, between the enduring changes which result from a different socialization and the revolt which is a phase of adolescence and passes when the youngster leaves his teens.

Women as well as men have a broad range of possible modes of life to choose from — at least theoretically — in cultures in which there is an ideology of equality. They may marry or not, have children or not, work or not; and if they do choose to work they may select whatever jobs or careers suit their talents and temperaments. Few American women, however, have successfully combined the seeming obligations of their femi-

[6] Alex Inkeles, "Social Change and Social Character: The Role of Parental Meditation," *Journal of Social Issues* 11, No. 2 (1955), 12–22.

[7] Cf. Kingsley Davis, "The Sociology of Parent-Youth Conflict," *American Sociological Review* 4 (1940), 523–535.

nine roles with their occupational and professional roles. This failure is a direct consequence of the cultural image of the female sex-role which forms a major impediment in socialization to a new, alternate image. The traditional image is often so dominant that it obscures the reality, which is that one may, in fact, combine these roles. A dramatic example of the lack of models available to the young girl is Betty Friedan's observation that aside from women who were wives and mothers, "The only other kind of women I knew, growing up, were the old-maid high-school teachers; the librarian; the one woman doctor in our town, who cut her hair like a man; and a few of my college professors. . . . I never knew a woman, when I was growing up, who used her mind, played her own part in the world, and also loved, and had children." [8]

The lack of motivational models for the girl, either in life or in fiction, has become a matter of concern to educators, some of whom have begun to translate the need into proposals for action. One has stated: "If the predictions are accurate that women are and will be needed to fill society's needs for highly qualified talent, it may be that the University will have to give more thought to *providing models for the undergraduate women by employing more women faculty members in prestige positions to demonstrate that such fields are open to qualified women.*" [9] The importance of role models and the deleterious effect of their absence on the motivation of young women has been stressed, not only by educators interested in women's greater participation in professional careers, but also by many lay observers. In an article on Indira Gandhi for *Harper's Bazaar*, Natalie Gittelson writes of a mother of teen-age daughters who commented, "At last my daughters will have a heroine who is brave as well as beautiful and dedicated to something more than the pursuit of self." [10]

Yet it is questionable whether isolated examples of promi-

[8] Betty Friedan, *The Feminine Mystique*, p. 75.

[9] Dorothy Robinson Ross, "The Story of the Top 1 Percent of the Women at Michigan State University," mimeographed, p. 80.

[10] Natalie Gittelson, "Her Excellency, the Prime Minister," *Harper's Bazaar* (June 1966), p. 100.

nent women can serve as models for many young women. It is true that the ascendancy of Indira Gandhi to the leadership of India at least establishes that "it can be done," but whether hers remains an idiosyncratic case for India, as with Sirimavo Bandaranaike in Ceylon, or the beginning of a trend in the world, remains to be seen.

Thus, although there are some women who do achieve a successful combination role and serve as models for the young, few positive examples exist in American society, and role models remain a limited agent of socialization for America's young women.

Formal Education

It is important to consider that women receive formal educations which are nearly comparable in content with those that men receive, certainly up to and often including their college years. But let us look at the duration of education. Many girls do not make it to college simply because they are girls; their brothers of equal ability are encouraged to continue beyond high school. The low percentage of women in professional positions requiring advanced training reflects the shrinking of the pool of available skilled womanpower at this level. Although there are more girls than boys in high school graduation classes, more boys than girls graduate from college, a pattern unchanged since the start of the century, as Table 5 indicates.

One of the principal successes of American education has been the increased number of young people, both men and women, who receive higher education. Today about 40 percent of college graduates are women, not too far from half, after all — about the same proportion as in 1930 and certainly an improvement over the 1950's (see Table 6). But other countries are catching up. Today the proportion of women educated in the United States relative to men is little greater than it is in a number of other countries, and even where the proportion is lower, there are many indications that the gap is being closed.

At the close of the nineteenth century, one-third of Ameri-

TABLE 5

High School and College Graduates (Bachelor's Degree) by Sex (U.S. 1900-1965)
(percentage in parentheses)

Year of graduation	High school		College (B.A. Degree)	
	Males	Females	Males	Females
1900	38,075 (40.1)	56,808 (59.9)	22,175 (80.9)	5,237 (19.1)
1940	587,718 (47.7)	642,757 (52.3)	109,546 (58.7)	76,954 (41.3)
1950	570,700 (47.5)	629,000 (52.5)	328,841 (76.1)	103,217 (23.9)
1960	898,000 (48.2)	966,000 (51.8)	254,063 (64.7)	138,377 (35.3)
1965	1,303,000 (49.4)	1,337,000 (50.6)	317,669 (59.3)	217,362 (40.7)

Source: *Statistical Abstract of the United States, 1967*, Table 184, p. 131.

TABLE 6

College and University Degrees Earned by Women
(United States)

Degree Conferred	Percent Earned by Women					
	1966	1965	1960	1950	1930	1900
Total	38.4	38.5	34.2	24.4	39.5	18.9
Bachelor's (or first professional)	40.4	40.7	35.3	23.9	39.9	19.1
Master's	33.8	32.1	31.6	29.2	40.4	19.1
Doctor's	11.6	10.8	10.5	9.7	15.4	6.0

Source: *1968 Handbook of Women Workers*, Washington, D.C., U.S. Department of Labor, Women's Bureau, draft, forthcoming.

can college students were women; by 1937, women made up almost 40 percent of the students in American institutions of higher learning. In Germany, just before Hitler took power, no more than one out of ten university students was a woman; in Swedish universities in 1937, only 17 percent of the students were women; in British universities at that time, the ratio was 22 percent; and in the Soviet Union in 1939, women comprised 32.1 percent of university students. But since World War II, the gap between the proportions of American and European women in higher education has narrowed considerably. In 1960, women constituted only 35 percent of the American college population, while France counted women as 38 percent of its university students and Sweden 33 percent, and in 1959 the U.S.S.R. 48.8 percent.[11] In 1963, in the United States and Great Britain women constituted 39 percent of college students. The U.S.S.R. had gone to 43 percent (a decrease since the previous decade).[12]

The dropout picture in college also provides clues to the low

[11] Carl N. Degler, "Revolution Without Ideology: The Changing Place of Women in America," *Daedalus* (Spring 1964), pp. 662–663.
[12] *UNESCO Statistical Yearbook, 1965* (New York: Unesco Publishing Center, 1966), pp. 249–265.

percentage of women in professional work. The college drop-out ratio is the same for both sexes: four out of every ten who enter.[13] The reasons, however, are different. Boys are more likely to leave school because of academic difficulties or problems of personal adjustment. The most frequent reason given by girls was marriage. They drop out at higher rates than men in professional training, however, and of course there are large percentages of able women who don't drop out because they didn't enter in the first place.

Studies show that in the United States fewer gifted women than gifted men even enter college:[14] about half of the brightest 40 percent of high school graduates go on to college; of the half who stay away, two-thirds are women. More gifted women than gifted men drop out, according to a study of the National Merit Scholarship Corporation. Almost 14 percent of the women compared with 9 percent of the men who scored high on the 1957 National Merit Scholarship qualifying test left school; relatively more women who attend physical science and professional programs drop out than men.[15] The National Merit Scholarship report also noted that those women who attend a college with a large number of male students, particularly one stressing engineering and business, drop out in greater proportion than those at other kinds of institutions. A report by Dr. Elizabeth McGrew of the University of Illinois College of Medicine showed that 10 percent of the college's dropouts were women although women constituted only 5 percent of the student body.[16]

As one climbs the ladder of American higher education, the proportion of all women steadily declines. (See Table 7.) The

[13] *Population Profile, 1964,* (Washington, D.C.: Population Reference Bureau, June 1, 1964), p. 2.
[14] Robert Sutherland, "Some Basic Facts," in Opal D. David (ed.), *The Education of Women,* p. 14.
[15] Alexander W. Austin, *New York Times* (November 2, 1964).
[16] Elizabeth McGrew, M.D., et al., "Medical Womanpower: Can It Be Used More Effectively?" *Journal of the American Medical Women's Association* 17 (December 1962), 973–985.

TABLE 7

Percent of Men and Women Receiving B.A. and Professional Degrees, 1964-65
(IN: inapplicable)

	B.A.		M.A.		Ph.D.[a]	
	Male	Female	Male	Female	Male	Female
All fields	56.7	43.3	67.9	32.1	89.2	10.8
Biological sciences	70.7	29.3	72.9	27.1	88.0	12.0
Engineering	99.6	0.4	99.6	0.4	99.5	0.5
Physical sciences	85.8	14.2	89.5	10.5	95.5	4.5
Dentistry (1st professional)	99.2	0.8	IN	IN	IN	IN
Medicine, M.D. only (1st professional)	93.4	6.6	IN	IN	IN	IN
Law[b] (1st professional)	99.6	3.4	96.7	3.2	93.1	6.9

Source: The National Center for Educational Statistics, "Summary Report on bachelor's and higher degrees conferred during the year 1964-65" (Washington: U.S. Government Printing Office, 1966), Table 4, pp. 4-9.

[a] The base figures on which the Ph.D. percentages were computed are, in some instances quite small, e.g. in law 27 for males and only 2 for females.

[b] For Law B.A., percentages were 95.6, Male; and 4.4, Female.

percentage of women applying to medical school is lower than it was ten to fifteen years ago.[17] Women's share of college degrees of all sorts, which had risen from 19 percent at the turn of the century to almost 41 percent just before World War II, slid back considerably during the 1950's but returned to the earlier level in the mid-1960's. In 1965, women received only one in eleven of the Ph.D.'s offered, however.[18]

Ambiguity of Socialization in School Years

The deterrence pattern is present in the earliest socialization of the young girl, and she grows up in an environment poor in

[17] *Ibid.*

[18] Margaret Mead and Francis Kaplan (eds.), *American Women* (New York: Charles Scribner's Sons, 1965), p. 27.

models and ideals other than those which are oriented on the career-home axis. Although her training is far from discontinuous — many sociologists have believed it to be sporadic — at each step she is exposed to ambiguous expectations and her training for any one role is seriously undermined by her training for others. Betty Friedan vividly describes the issue:

The strange, terrifying jumping-off point that American women reach — at eighteen, twenty-one, twenty-five, forty-one — has been noticed for years by sociologists, psychologists, analysts, educators. But I think it has not been understood for what it is. It has been called a "discontinuity" in cultural conditioning; it has been called woman's "role crisis." It has been blamed on the education which made American girls grow up feeling free and equal to boys — playing baseball, riding bicycles, conquering geometry and college boards, going away to college, going out in the world to get a job, living alone in an apartment in New York or Chicago or San Francisco, testing and discovering their own powers in the world. All this gave girls the feeling they could be and do whatever they wanted to, with the same freedom as boys, the critics said. It did not prepare them for their role as women. The crisis comes when they are forced to adjust to this role. Today's women's high rate of emotional distress and breakdown in their twenties and thirties is usually attributed to this "role crisis." If girls were educated for their role as women, they would not suffer this crisis, the adjusters say.[19]

The young girl is asked to be studious and learn, but she increasingly becomes aware that she may not be asked to demonstrate her knowledge. She is asked to be good-looking, and charming and deferential to men, yet she must go to school and compete with young men at all levels of educational training. The syndrome has a variety of labels, like cultural discontinuity or identity stress. Here is where social structural ambiguity or sociological ambivalence come in.

[19] Friedan, op. cit., p. 75.

It is not easy to isolate all the contradictory messages intelligent young women get from their environment about expectations for their future. The primary message, of course, is that in order to be "women," they must seek marriage and children. Also, they are asked to perform well in school and *perhaps* later on in some job.

In the Aberle and Naegele study cited previously, over half of the fathers accepted the possibility of a career for their daughters, although their first concern was that their daughters marry. The other half rejected a career for their girls out of hand.[20]

All arrows direct the girl to marriage. We do not need to document this or back it up with opinion polls or attitude studies. In fact, there is probably no society in the world which does not stress marriage as the primary objective of the overwhelming majority of its young women, exception made for the small number of women recruited into religious orders. Men face the marriage mandate too, but, though marriage is implicitly emphasized as a requisite for manhood, marriage itself is not seen as a goal, a limiting factor, or a state excluding the man's other role commitments. Men marry and seek happiness by challenging the world; for women, however, it is enough to marry and to live happily ever after. The emphasis on being a wife first and foremost has many consequences for the girl's behavior at all stages of development and at all points in her preparation for a career when a decision must be made.

A number of studies document the effect of marriage socialization on talented women in American society. Super found that intellectually superior twelfth-grade girls were more "marriage-oriented" than "work-oriented."[21] Super[22] noted in his study of occupations that women saw themselves as helpers — nurses and secretaries — rather than as leaders or creators.

[20] Aberle and Naegele, *op. cit.*, p. 100.
[21] Donald E. Super, *Career Development: Self-Concept Theory* (New York College Entrance Examination Board, 1963).
[22] Donald E. Super, *Psychology of Careers* (New York: Harper and Brothers, 1957), p. 294.

Friedman's report on Vassar students in 1956 indicated that marriage at graduation or within a few years was anticipated by almost all students. Strong commitment to any activity or career other than that of housewife was rare; few planned to continue with a career if it would conflict with family needs. Compared with women students of the feminist era, for example, he felt that few of these students were interested in the pursuit of demanding careers such as law or medicine.[23]

In a study of overachievement and underachievement among high school students,[24] it was found that underachieving girls' grades dropped at the onset of puberty, while boys who were underachievers showed a disposition to lower performance very early in their elementary school careers. This raises the possibility that the problems of playing out the sexual role encountered at puberty were of great relevance to the girls' underachievement. Further, girls with high grades were rated by their same-sex peers as being less acceptable to boys than girls with lower grades.[25]

Not only is academic achievement undercut, but general involvement with academic work is undermined by the emphasis on the girl's future role as wife. Girls do not seem to be encouraged to make their work part of their identity, as men later do. Paravocational hobbies are not stressed (boys get chemistry sets, girls get make-up kits).

Helen Hacker notes: "Because women have been trained to set greater store on personal characteristics than on accomplishments, their work lacks the performance orientation of men . . . they receive mainly ascriptive rewards — the glamour of being a working woman. Their lack of achievement rewards is documented . . . we find so few women saying they work because they enjoy their jobs or work for the work's

[23] Mervin Friedman, "The Passage Through College," *Journal of Social Issues* 12, No. 4 (1956), 13–28.
[24] David E. Lavin, *The Prediction of Academic Performance* (New York: Russell Sage Foundation, 1965), p. 130.
[25] *Ibid.*, p. 135.

sake." [26] And Davis and Oleson point to anxiety experienced by nursing students whose vocational commitment — even in this "female-defined" occupation — conflicts with their emerging identity of adult womanhood.[27] Career skills have to be developed early. Even if these skills are to be held in reserve, the decision must be made before marriage as to how much and what level or quality of training should be undertaken. Bettelheim has observed: ". . . boys have no doubt that their schooling is intended, at least, to help them make a *success* in their mature life, to enable them to accomplish something in the outside world. But the girl is made to feel that she must undergo precisely the same training only because she may need it if she is a *failure* — an unfortunate who somehow cannot gain admission to the haven of marriage and motherhood where she properly belongs. Surely this is absurd." [28]

Girls may become confused when they hear contradictory messages from family and teachers to train (but not be emotionally committed to the training) and to prepare for their future family role (but become involved in the educational process and compete there with young men). Perhaps it is because parents themselves do not know how strongly they feel about each of these messages and cannot clarify their stand that the girl feels they say one thing at one time and another thing at another. Ross's findings corroborate Mirra Komarovsky's earlier study [29] of Barnard students. They are illustrated by the comment of one girl in the Ross sample: "First my parents encourage me to get grades, and then they worry I'm not meeting any boys or having any fun. When I do go out and have fun, they worry about my grades. I feel pulled two ways." [30] Has this changed in two decades? Mirra Komarovsky has reported

[26] Hacker dissertation, *op. cit.*, chapter 1, p. 5.

[27] Fred Davis and Virginia L. Oleson, "Initiation into a Woman's Profession: Identity Problems in the Status Transition of Coed to Student Nurse," *Sociometry* 26 (March 1963), 89.

[28] Bettelheim, "Growing Up Female," *Harper's* (October 1962), p. 121.

[29] Mirra Komarovsky, "Cultural Contradictions and Sex Roles," *American Journal of Sociology* 52, No. 6 (November 1946), 184–189.

[30] Ross, *op. cit.*, pp. 23–24.

to me that she finds Barnard students in 1968 are still in conflict over whether they should select kinds of work which require postgraduate training (a majority of Barnard graduates do go on to graduate training). Placement directors at Barnard and at other leading women's colleges report the same thing. These college women's plans for the future are highly contingent and subject to modification because of plans of spouses or future spouses. Even these able and well-educated girls abandon their own plans if they feel they ought to work to support a husband during his specialized training or if he chooses to work somewhere where training is not available to her. From observations and discussions at a recent conference at Bennington College, it was clear that most women at this high-prestige institution do not care to undertake professional and graduate education as a step toward career preparation. They have no future image of themselves as working women. They also reject the image of homemaker, but perhaps this is because it is not fashionable there to wish openly to become the wife of a doctor, lawyer, or corporation executive (most, in fact, do become wives of such men). Their rejection of both alternatives indicates that they have no clear visualization of the future, and thus do not prepare themselves for what is to come. The talents of these girls, which find expression within the college community and through the college years, die on the vine, since reality orientation seems to be absent. At Queens College, part of the City University of New York, most women students of middle- and lower-class background whom I have interviewed seem to opt for one of the most traditional of women's roles — to teach in public school in the years between graduation and marriage. Almost 95 percent of the girls in my classes during the past two years have chosen this as the best course open to them.

Motivation to go to college and motivation to use college training do not seem to be linked. Getting a college education is now a middle-class imperative,[31] and girls seem to do well at it,

---

[31] William H. Whyte perceptively observed that it was not very important for a corporation wife to have gone to college, but it is very important for her

at the very least because their early docility training stands them in good stead in the discipline of performing assignments and following instructors' cues. Just as in school, their middle-class fathers expect and want them to perform well, part of a generalized desire to have good girls who are sexually moral, nice, and sweet.[32] But the college does not necessarily take the performance of a young woman as an indicator of later productiveness in the occupational world, and it is probably true that informal sex quotas are maintained for fellowships and scholarships. It is also probably true that senior professors do not groom young women as disciples or successors, though they utilize their skills as assistants. (Social complications can arise from a close working relationship between professor and female student; and the professor may feel loath to pursue such in involvement.) [33] Even if this kind of discrimination does not occur, women often anticipate it. They may, as a consequence, never enter competition for awards which they might have had.

A young woman is usually aware that by trying harder she may be labeled "hard-driving" and "ambitious," positive attributes for a man but pejorative descriptions of a woman overstepping the boundaries of preferred behavior.

Seldom do even educated girls hold a mental picture of a family basking in the reflected glow of the mother's achievement as a scientist or judge if she is not also portrayed as a good homemaker. No one asks if a male Nobel Prize winner is also a good father; whether or not he even has children is probably irrelevant to his biography. But the headline on a recent article about a female Nobel laureate scientist read, "Grandmother Wins Award," [34] as if having grandchildren had some relevance to high professional achievement.

---

not to have *not* gone to college. "The Wife Problem," *Life* (January 7, 1952), cited in Winch, McGinnis, and Baringer (eds.), *Selected Studies in Marriage and the Family* (New York: Holt, Rinehart, and Winston, 1962), p. 119.

[32] Aberle and Naegele, *op. cit.*, p. 103.

[33] A further analysis of the apprentice relationship follows in Chapter IV.

[34] Reference to the fact that Nobel Prize winner Dorothy C. Hodgkin was a grandmother was prominent in the *New York Times* article announcing the award, October 30, 1964.

Donald Brown's study of a group of superior female college students showed that they had little motivation in *any* direction. He found there was:

Little to indicate that the subjects as a group had deep interests that they pursued with vigor in their spare time. Rather, their activities tended to be scattered and fragmented: for example, if they read a lot, they read about many topics in a fairly superficial manner. They were rarely expert in anything. American women, whether educated or not, do not often find themselves in a situation where they can become deeply involved in interests of their own.[35]

A further problem arises when all expectations, contradictory or not, are accepted as legitimate. A study by Rose indicates that because women expect to do everything, they may in fact be unrealistic in their planning and their time budgeting may limit them on all fronts. He showed that women's expectations about their role-time budget as adults were overascribed and unrealistic, and that role conflict was assured if they attempted to fulfill all expectations. Rose summarizes his findings, saying

. . . that practically all women expect to raise children and spend a good deal of time on them and housework. We have also seen that most women expect to get a job and carry on with it past the birth of their children. Finally, we have seen that women expect to be at least as active as men in leisure time work, and that in civic and social welfare work alone they plan to spend an average of about ten hours a week. The whole adds up to too much. In addition, the data indicate that the average woman wants to, and even expects to, play every kind of social role. Even as late as her college years — when she is acquiring her last formal training for adulthood — her planning is not specific and tries to take in more than she will have time for. Either she will not be able to do all the things she expects to do, or her estimate of the amount of time she will need for housework and child-raising is unrealistically high.

[35] Donald Brown, "Some Educational Patterns," *Journal of Social Issues* 12 (4), 1956, pp. 44–60.

In either case her adult role is not yet clear to her at the college-student age.[36]

In Rose's study, more uncertainty about expectations was found among upper-class women. More gave "don't know" responses when asked the specific vocation they were training for, although as large a proportion of women as men said they expected to work after college. The poorer women of his sample were planning as carefully as men.[37]

What happens to aspiration under such conditions of ambiguity and ambivalence?

Reporting on the top 1 percent of female students at Michigan State College for 1958 and 1962, Dorothy Ross outlined a number of mechanisms by which young women coped with this situation. The group queried in 1958 tended to "avoid" any problem by keeping their abilities hidden. Ross reported that the women demonstrated a reluctance to reveal their superior potential. This was seen as stemming from a need to protect themselves against the possibility of peer-group rejection, particularly rejection by the male students. The 1962 sample showed a change. Girls in this group initiated a contact with the school newspaper which brought their achievement before the student public's eye. But without more data it is hard to say whether this switch was idiosyncratic or constituted a real trend. Ross also collected interviews which indicated anxieties ranging from purely academic concern about maintaining a high level of achievement to ". . . conflict caused by what they felt was ambiguity in the expectations of their parents or other significant adults to maximize their academic potential and also make successful marriages," and ". . . anxiety over their finding a mate — not just any mate, but one who was their equal or superior." Of the group entering in 1958, 68 percent expressed a desire to go on

[36] Arnold Rose, "The Adequacy of Woman's Expectations for Adult Roles," *Social Forces* 30, No. 6 (1951), 69–77.
[37] *Ibid.*

to graduate or professional school; in 1962, 81 percent of the entering class indicated that they were planning some combination of graduate school, career, and marriage. But even with the increase in the career-oriented group, in both years concern was manifest about the ability to combine marriage with career aspirations.[38]

It would be interesting to know what percentage of the young women who voiced doubts did go on to a career; we might see to what extent the early doubts acted as a self-fulfilling prophecy. Anticipation of problems and expectations of ultimate defeat probably do result in weak commitment to any career goal, lessened investment in training, and perhaps less toleration of early deprivations which would make success more possible.

The Tendency to Choose "Female" Occupations

What happens if a young American woman really wants a career? Even assuming high motivation for a career on the part of young women, or readiness to see the future as having room for both a family and some kind of work, few women actually choose the scientific and professional fields. Not only can we note the tiny percentages of women in these fields but there seems to be a sifting-out process in the career decisions of gifted students, men tending to graduate in the sciences and women in the social sciences and humanities. The Ross study of the Michigan girls showed that by graduation most of those who originally opted for the sciences had switched to those fields considered extensions of the female role — social work, nursing, teaching, and home economics; those women majoring in these fields increased from 60 percent to 83 percent. But even with this change, the majority still had no specific career plans to which they were committed as lifetime goals.[39]

A 1962 Department of Labor survey showed that the subjects in which the largest numbers of men earned their degrees were

[38] Ross, *op. cit.*, p. 23.　　　[39] *Ibid.*, p. 73.

quite different from those chosen by women, except for an overlapping area in the social sciences. The three most popular
undergraduate majors for men were business and commerce
(19 percent), engineering (15 percent), and social sciences (14
percent). Ten percent of the men receiving bachelor's degrees
specialized in education and 36 percent of those receiving mas-
ter's degrees. Women received almost all the degrees in home
economics and nursing and about three-fourths of those in library science. A majority of women opted for education, English, journalism, and foreign languages. Men received at least
nine-tenths of the degrees in engineering, agriculture, law, medicine, and business and commerce; almost nine-tenths in the
physical sciences and pharmacy; and about three-fourths of
those in the biological sciences and mathematics.[40]

In contrast, in Swedish universities for the same period
women made up a quarter of the students of medicine, dentistry, and the natural sciences, and 15 percent of those in law
schools; a majority of the pharmacy students are women.[41]

There have been some minor changes in percentages since
1962. In 1964, for example, fewer women were interested in education because they were branching into other fields, such as
speech correction.[42]

An even more startling contrast is provided by a recently reported study of Soviet youngsters of 15 and 16 years of age regarding their career plans. In this study, 20 percent of the girls
(of a total of 1,114) chose to become doctors while only 1.2 percent (of 763) of the boys opted for this occupation. Girls also
led boys in choices to become agronomists and veterinarians
and about one hundred girls expressed the wish to take training which would give them careers as pilots, motor vehicle op-
erators, and geologists. The findings of this study are particularly impressive since the study was done of youth in rural

[40] *Handbook of Women Workers, 1962*, U.S. Department of Labor, Women's
Bureau Bulletin 285.
   [41] Tomasson, "The Swedes Do It Better," p. 179.
   [42] "1968 Handbook of Women Workers," U.S. Department of Labor, forthcoming.

areas where one might expect more traditional attitudes toward appropriate careers for women.[43]

Problems in Education and Training

What are the elements in training and the structure of training which facilitate or hinder a woman's commitment to professional life? Many of the same factors affect both men and women and, depending on their personalities and abilities, they may find that training per se is no problem or that it does not match their expectations and hence is extremely difficult.

Many of the issues of talent and education are relevant for both boys and girls. Whether our concern is the so-called challenge of education, conformity, the aims of college training, dropouts, or achievement motivation, boys as well as girls clearly do not explore their full potential. But the context of the training acts differentially on men and women, especially where women find themselves a distinct minority or majority. For women, their sex itself becomes a different context within which these variables operate.

Access to educational opportunities now is assured to women as well as men with only a few limitations.[44] Why are they underutilized by women? Some elements of other societies' educational systems can throw light on drawbacks in professional orientation in our country. Again, men as well as women are affected by these strictures, but taking account of women's greater dependence on a supportive and channeling structure (as we are hypothesizing), they seem especially relevant for women.

[43] F. N. Rekunov and N. A. Shlapak, "The Career Plans of Graduates of Rural Schools," *Soviet Education* 11, No. 3–4–5 (January–February–March 1969), 104–115. These findings are reported in Table I, "Occupations Chosen by Graduating Students of Rural Eight-Year Schools (Based on Questionnaires Submitted to Students in Sverdlovsk Region and in the Trans-Baikal, 1964–5)," p. 105.

[44] Free access is limited to some extent in terms of quotas in professional schools, but it is very difficult to ascertain what the quotas are and to what extent there are *any* quotas.

SPECIALIZATION

In some European and Latin American countries and in the Soviet Union, at the point at which higher education begins the student must commit himself to a specialty. Thus, at the equivalent of the college freshman year, the student already begins premedical, engineering, or other specialized studies. Although one may argue the benefit of the broad liberal arts education common in the United States, there is no doubt that many students complete this kind of education and obtain degrees without having acquired any vocational training or marketable skills. Thus, American college girls (even those from "better" schools) seeking their first job often must become secretaries or trainees for relatively low-level, dead-end jobs. With specialized training, however, it is easier to get a first job and to commit to a career because of time invested in training. A number of researchers have noted that an interval of time devoted to training for an occupation often represents an investment in students' eyes. Thielens reports this for law students; Becker and Carper report that graduate physiology and philosophy students considered each successive semester of study an increasing investment in this sense, and felt increasing pressure to continue in the career and to develop work identification with it, to avoid the loss of this investment. Ginzberg and his associates also discussed the "irreversibility" of the occupational entry process inherent in the investment of time required by education and training.[45]

It also is easier to resign oneself to not working when the opportunities are poor and the work is less demanding than it is when one is able to work in a job that will tap one's talents and training, whether as engineer or librarian. When I recently asked a woman lawyer what her plans would be if she were

[45] Wagner Thielens, Jr., "The Development of an Occupational Self-Image," Part III of "The Socialization of Law Students, A Case Study in Three Parts," unpub. Ph.D. diss. (Columbia University, 1965), pp. 270–297. Howard S. Becker and James W. Carper, "The Development of Identification with an Occupation," *American Journal of Sociology* 61 (January 1956), 296. Eli Ginzberg *et al.*, *Occupational Choice*, pp. 193–196.

forced to leave her present position she commented: "Frankly it would depend on whether I could get another job. I don't intend to hit my head against a stone wall for the next five years. This is probably why so many women leave law."

Women's withdrawal rates from occupations vary, according to the little evidence we have. Alice Rossi, using National Opinion Research Center data, has found that women engineers and scientists show a moderately high rate of withdrawal (51 percent) from their occupations in the 22–44 age group, according to a NORC study,[46] possibly as a result of the active discrimination against them in those male-dominated fields. But women teachers also drop out with some frequency (34 percent) possibly because of the lower commitment on the part of teachers to remaining in the labor force. Women doctors, however, have low withdrawal rates compared with women in other fields, Of course the male drop-out rates also vary from field to field. In those fields in which men's rates are low — medicine, for example — women's also tend to be low, although the percentages of withdrawal are always higher than men's.

SUPPORT FOR TRAINING

Because of state support of training in some countries (for example, medicine in Great Britain and college training generally in the Soviet Union), the student often is required to work for a specified number of years at government-assigned jobs, partly as repayment for society's investment in the student. This means that the graduate is guaranteed a job, is spared the frustrations of job hunting, and must work at what he is trained for, barring a very valid excuse. (While a woman might be given special dispensation if she is pregnant, there is no doubt that there are definite pressures on her to fulfill her obligations, both morally and contractually.) Working immediately in one's own field reinforces the commitment, starts the person in his career, and makes the rewards (and drawbacks)

[46] Rossi, "Women in Science, Why So Few?" *Science* (May 28, 1965), p. 1196.

real. At the level of professional work, the first years are probably crucial to establishing the self-image [47] and "hooking" the
incumbent. Even if the person leaves a field for a time, he or
she has a better chance to reenter than to start in a field years
after training has been completed. Many who have advised
American women on careers have suggested that they at least
complete their training and obtain whatever certification is required before taking a leave of absence for childbirth. In any
event, the absence of such pressures in American society acts
against women's work commitment.

Pressures on Women to Work

American society's conflicting messages to women have been
examined, yet we have stressed only those encouraging marriage and good school performance. There are, however, socialization processes at work which direct women into occupations
or peripheral work of some sort, for example, pressures for the
use of women's intellect for the benefit of the community in
charitable work on a nonpaying basis. In addition, women are
asked to consider working for pay to augment the family's income and to fill their later years when children are grown.
This means that motivation for women develops in another
context than the one in which men are socialized to work. It occurs within a contingency spectrum.

Contingency Planning

A young man starts thinking early about work because he
knows he will be responsible for earning an income for himself
and his family, and because as an adult he will be measured by
the work he produces. A woman may start thinking about
working because a man let her down. It may be because of a
need for supplementary income if a husband's income is not

[47] Wagner Thielens, Jr., "Some Comparisons of Entrants to Medical and
Law School," Merton, Reader, and Kendall (eds.), *The Student-Physician.*
Also, Warkov and Zelan, *Lawyers in the Making*, and Wagner Thielens, Jr.,
unpublished dissertation, *op. cit.*

viewed as adequate; or because of a need for emergency income if he should be unemployed, disabled, or die. For the most part, these situations are more likely to occur in the lower strata of society, where layoffs or continuous low income are real problems. In the upper strata, women are less subject to the fears of such an eventuality and to the notion that it is their responsibility to prepare for it. Even where crises occur, solutions for them are sought in other ways than the wife's entering the job market (indeed, this prospect probably ranks lowest on the priority scale): insurance is one answer; another is an alternate breadwinner, a father or father-in-law or older son. Women at the top economic levels, the ones who form the pool from which we might expect to draw the highest percentages of professionals (since they alone have the resources for the long training for professional work), are subject to the least economic pressure and possess none of the norms prescribing what work to seek or do.

Even where it is routinely expected that a young girl will take a job when first out of high school or college, she usually is not expected to carve out a career or rise to a position of wealth and power. Women inherit wealth, they seldom make it, and the woman who does make it is considered something of an oddity. There are few norms relating to interaction with women "achievers" outside the traditionally female-defined areas — few enough to make for discomfort and to make necessary a new set of ground rules. Many men would rather see women retreat from the realms where they do not know how to act with her than make adjustments to her presence.[48] Even in the Jewish *shtetl* communities of eastern Europe, where married women's work was institutionalized and families often depended on the woman as sole breadwinner of the family,[49] it was clearly understood she did so as handmaiden to a scholarly

---

[48] Goode presents an analogous case in the pressures on the divorced woman by her friends to remarry, since they find it difficult to include a single woman in their social life, which is based on pairs of married couples, *Women in Divorce.*

[49] Zborowski and Herzog, *Life Is with People,* p. 240.

husband for whom learning was the cherished career and whom she was serving in the hope of sitting at his feet in heaven.

It is important to stress that although there are factors of reality which deflect women from choosing careers, the socialization process works on the woman in such a way that she often decides against a career without actually testing reality. Rather, she anticipates consequences and accepts limitations or a defeat which may not be inevitable in her case. Paralleling the psychological mechanisms of avoidance and denial, women (like members of other minority groups who remain in their ghettos) accept defeat rather than face the battle. David Riesman has remarked on the self-defeating consequences of preparing for a narrow existing reality, comparing women's hesitancy in pursuing demanding careers with the Negro pattern:

... Negro colleges like Tuskegee ... said to their students: "There's no chance for Negro engineers, Negro technicians and professionals in a dozen fields where they would be in the same pyramid with whites; so we've got to turn out Negro mechanics, artisans, and agriculturists, for which there will always be a market." ... Today, one finds many places that would like to hire a Negro anesthetist or engineer or psychologist, but not enough Negroes took chances a generation ago on an "impractical" education to be available for these places which now unexpectedly exist: hence, the sound practical earlier judgment turns out to be self-confirming, like so much work in the field of vocational guidance.[50]

In fact, the whole process of preparation for reality may miscarry as women fail to raise their sights — and training — to meet the new realities that will exist within their working lives. But we do not prepare ourselves for changing times. Riesman also observes that "an education which seeks to avoid discontent by avoiding discontinuity between college and 'life' is ac-

[50] Riesman, "Some Continuities and Discontinuities in the Education of Women," Third John Dewey Memorial Lecture, Bennington College, Bennington, Vermont, June 7, 1956, p. 14.

tually maladaptive as well as patronizing." [51] These limiting and self-limiting mechanisms operate not only at the earliest stages of women's career decisions, but throughout their lives.

Differential Socialization

Dominant modes of socialization are comparatively flexible and permit a variety of behavior, but still may be completely inappropriate for some women. This should lead to the appearance of changing roles, or deviant behavior.

Spinsters are more and more a dying breed, and most young women dream of life with a husband. But if a young woman feels that a husband will not appear, or if there is a limited pool of eligible men, her thinking about a career may take a different course from that of her sisters. This constitutes another form of contingency planning.

During World War II, for instance, when the young men were off at war, dating did not consume the time of the college co-ed and she redirected her energies to study. The paucity of dates also raised uncertainty in the hearts of young women, for it was likely they might not marry for some time and, indeed, might not marry at all. Work became an alternative even for those who did marry. Once engaged in an occupation, many had so firm a foothold they were loath to give it up.

Even in normal times there are young women who are not exposed to directly contradictory messages from their elders and models. One might expect that young women with mothers who are professionals and thus positive role models will see that pursuing both career and motherhood is possible. And working mothers who enjoy what they are doing emanate positive messages to their daughters. (We should note that the only two fathers who wanted their daughters to have careers in the Aberle and Naegele study had wives who had worked or were working during their married lives.) [52] We may also find a general relaxation of status definition in times of social

[51] *Ibid.*, p. 15.
[52] Aberle and Naegele, *op. cit.*, p. 102.

change, or in cases where the mobility of a given family causes
it to experience internal social change. Early influences en-
hancing a girl's motivation to work may come from a family
which is not rooted in the status quo and is free from society's
classic notions about women's place and the sex division of
labor. Thus, immigrant parents might be more apt to encourage daughters to try a new way, and to find a better life in the
new world, than old-stock American parents who are rooted in
the structure as it is or who are too tradition-bound to expect
change. Such was the immigrant background of many women
lawyers in my study who were between 40 and 50 years of age.
The same would be true for lower-stratum parents with aspirations to move higher in the economic scale, because they know
the old way is the poor way and they might be willing to urge
something new on their children.

Placement in the Family Structure

The woman who has had a special place in her family probably is better able to avoid a stereotyped mold. Although birth-
order studies have been challenged,[53] some of the findings are
interesting in this context. A cursory look at biographies of
noted women in the news of recent years indicates a wide
range of birth-order positions: some have been only children
while others come from large families. The Ross data corroborate birth-order findings of earlier studies showing that first-
born or only children have higher I.Q.'s, are more creative, and
the like. Fourteen of sixteen women in the top 1 percent at
Michigan State University in 1958 were either only children or
eldest children.[54] Anne Roe's research about male scientists suggests that they too tend to be only children or first-born.[55] It
would be interesting to know if placement within the family is
of any consequence in determining whether or not a young

[53] The findings on birth order have been found contradictory and birth order
is not a powerful predictor.
[54] Ross, op. cit., p. 41.
[55] Anne Roe, The Psychology of Occupations (New York: John Wiley and
Sons, Inc., 1956).

woman will choose a career. Perhaps the qualities of the environment of first or only children are of greater consequence: isolation, a feeling of being special, perhaps a pace-setting quality.

Yet the consequence of being first-born might act against the future autonomy of the girl. Parents might be more apt to chart a known course for their first-born; and for women in most cases this would be a traditionally defined sex role. A younger daughter might be permitted and even encouraged to try something new; the older daughter might easily become a surrogate mother in her family, adhering to traditional family-centered expectations.[56] (For an older son to pursue a professional career, however, would be well in keeping with traditional expectations.) The younger daughter may have a real advantage in her quest for additional training for work; she often may be free from family responsibility, she may be more apt to be spoiled and indulged. If an older sister is present to carry on the role of the mother, the younger's rejection of a domestic role does not threaten anyone.

Ordinal position within the family may mean nothing, however, in the presence of other structural and psychological conditions. If the mother has been frustrated by her life as housewife, if the father chooses to exploit the daughter's talents in the absence of sons, if the family has an abundance of resources coupled with an ideology of service or productivity, then the girl, even if first-born, is not likely to be cornered in a traditional role and may have free rein to become a member of one of the professions if she wishes to do so. In fact, in such circumstances she may be pressured to do so.

Achievement-motivation studies have not usually reported

---

[56] A very recent study supports this notion. Kenneth Kammeyer found that first-born girls are more traditionally oriented toward the feminine role, have more traditional beliefs about female personality traits, are more likely to choose marriage over graduation from college, and are more likely to describe themselves as religious. They are also more likely to agree with their parents about the feminine role. "Birth Order and the Feminine Sex Role Among College Women," *American Sociological Review* 31 (1966), 508–515.

findings on women as they have on men, but it is likely that a different set of family dynamics is at play in the setting in which women, in contrast to men, acquire the motivation to work.

David McClelland finds that boys develop the need to achieve in a situation in which mother and son form a coalition and the mother presses her son to achieve (perhaps because of frustrated ambitions or disappointment in her husband) in an atmosphere of support and love.[57] The question then arising is what optimal family dynamic will cause the girl to focus on achievement. We might expect a coalition of father and daughter or a parallel coalition of mother and daughter (perhaps in the absence of a son). Some women lawyers interviewed for my study said they had been encouraged to become attorneys by mothers who were unable to fulfill ambitions for themselves. McClelland's research did not extend to girls, and no replication of his techniques has been done for young women. Hints of a pattern can be found in birth-order material and social-psychological data. Ross's observation[58] that "in some cases it was the father, in others the mother," who was the important influence on the child, indicates that no pattern or similar syndrome exists for the girl as it does for the boy. Stafford found that mothers and fathers were mentioned about equally as having influenced professional women listed in *Who's Who of American Women*.[59] It is probably true that whether the girl identifies more with the mother or the father, and then in turn whether the mother works, has ever worked, or has ever wished to work, has a great deal to do with which parent, if any, becomes a model for the girl. A girl who has identified with a housewife mother may simply adopt her mother as a model and never have career ambitions. Data from a yet un-

---

[57] See the body of research reported in David McClelland, *The Achieving Society*.

[58] Ross, *op. cit.*, p. 41.

[59] Rita Lynne Stafford, "An Analysis of Consciously Recalled Professional Involvement for American Women in New York State," unpublished Ph.D. dissertation, New York University, 1966.

published study of the relationship between parental characteristics and the educational plans of high school students indicate
that high school girls who plan to go on to college were less
likely to have been given chores to do by their mothers (suggesting that they were not channeled into female-role activities
early), and those who had "fun with their mothers" were less
likely to plan for college.[60]

Decision for college and a career beyond might not depend
on whether the mother or father were weak or strong. The girl
might simply be influenced by the mother to seek a mate with
more of the qualities of the ideal rather than to seek achievement on her own. And even if the girl identifies with a working mother she still is under strong pressure from the world
about her to conform to the many alternative models of womanly behavior in the classic hearth-and-home pattern. High
achievers in Brown's study ranked low in social-peer group oriented activity and "experienced conflicts in their early life and
adolescence, arising from domineering and talented
mothers. . . ." Brown's data indicate that alienation, when
coupled with ability and "intellectual activity from the earliest
years," might well permit orientation toward professional
roles.[61] But Havighurst found that girls with high achievement
scores were not as likely as boys who had high scores to go on
to college and he suggests that some girls with high achievement motivation satisfy this need vicariously through the career
of a husband.[62]

Other Motivating Conditions

Motivation toward professional roles may also arise where social changes make opportunities available for the first time and
the new jobs are not sex-typed.[63] New pathways become visi-

---

[60] Reported informally by study director Eva Sandis at the Bureau of Applied
Social Research, Columbia University.

[61] Brown, *op. cit.*, p. 54.

[62] Robert J. Havighurst, private communication, December 30, 1966, and
chapter 8 of his *Growing Up in River City*.

[63] See chapter 5, below.

ble; alternatives to the classic pattern are attractively presented and are most powerful under conditions in which women have little to lose. When change occurs concurrent with the emergence of an ideology of equality in the society, or idiosyncratically in families which treat daughters equally with sons, then we may expect women to have strong incentive and to plan for careers.

Brown's data show that high achievers most often come from public schools and from families which rarely were socially or intellectually prominent and in which the parents usually were not college-educated.[64] These were girls from families with no investment in tradition, girls who had much to gain in mobility by high academic achievement and professional commitment and were able to make use of new opportunities created by a more open educational system. There is a close relationship here to the motivation arising out of more distinct economic pressures (discussed below), which may or may not be linked to social change.

In American society, where living well is important and supposedly within the grasp of anyone who will work, economic pressures are often strong enough to push a family to send its women to work. Families may not intend their girls to become interested in lifetime careers, but careers may result from the exposure to work even in the absence of any strong early motivation. Women who enter the labor force without ever having thought of a career may continue to work past the point where economic need is primary, and then rise within the system.

These are the self-reinforcing mechanisms of work — exposure to a work situation which is engrossing to the woman, so rich with personal satisfaction and high economic rewards that she is seduced by it; or conversely, exposure to a routine work situation which offers a challenging higher level should the woman care for additional training.

As some men become rich simply by entering an industry

[64] Brown, *op. cit.*, p. 54.

whose growth is assured by the demands of an expanding economy, so some women may become professionals because of the growth of the enterprise with which they have become associated. They may find themselves growing into roles which have not been formally identified and assuming the identity (that is to say, formal assumption of the status) long after they have learned and performed the roles attached to the status. A large proportion of lawyers in my study began as legal secretaries. Many obtained their own law degrees long after they were in fact independently handling legal work (though they did not have clients). This may not be as idiosyncratic a process as it appears, for women often become assistants in situations in which they clearly have the potential and ability to perform independently. Since they cannot initially define themselves as professionals or professional trainees, the awareness may well occur after the fact, the reverse of the usual socializing process in professionalization.

Both men and women often find themselves in careers for which they do not have great incentive or motivation. Some choose a field because it appears to be better paying or attractive; others simply seem to drift or fall into a job and stay there. The latter is characteristic of lower-class boys who become factory workers. Some who enter the working world have the intention and desire to do a specific kind of work, for example, the young boy or girl who has always wanted to be a doctor or lawyer. Indeed, it is one of the characteristics of a profession that those who enter its ranks have a high emotional commitment to it. But one sees a pattern of drift even for entry to the professions, particularly in the process of selection of a specialty. In law, for instance, Carlin has pointed out that many practitioners discover themselves in specialties like matrimonial or negligence work, not by design, but because they have handled one or two cases successfully and find clients referring similar cases to them.[65] The economics of the legal marketplace

[65] Jerome Carlin, *Lawyers on Their Own.*

does not permit private practitioners to be choosy; in firms, lawyers may also have little choice of what kind of case is assigned to them.

Some professions and career occupations may lend themselves more to drift than others; motivation may thus be of greater intensity among members of one profession than another. Because training is long, and admittance to medical school requires planning and a high degree of personal input, it is likely that M.D. candidates are more highly motivated than those who choose to major in business administration. Every college student has to major in something, and the broader the base of ultimate career possibilities, the more candidates; it is possible to study business without a prior decision about how the training will be used. This phenomenon is peculiar to the American higher education system, since in European and Soviet universities students must specialize upon entering the university and begin immediate training for law, engineering, science, or another field of their choice.

We can assume that the woman who enters medical school has high motivation, that she doesn't simply drift into it. We might also assume that women who choose other professions are highly motivated to begin with, if not to the particular profession, then at least to the notion of being a professional person. Further data are needed to support these assumptions. It seems likely that women must be highly motivated to enter the professional world because the factors resisting their participation are strong. However, we must also expect them to be affected by the drift and self-reinforcing mechanisms characteristic of occupational participation in general.

Two other processes may affect women's orientation and motivation to work. In both the socialization directing them toward fulfillment of female sex roles channels them into work which is defined as an extension of these roles.

The first of these processes is illustrated by the situation in which a woman becomes involved in a career as an extension of feminine duty. It occurs where she begins work with a sense of obligation to aid a father or husband; thus a woman in a joint professional practice, even in a male-defined profession, may define and have her work defined as a helping — and therefore a female — role. Often in situations of this kind she does indeed do ancillary work: research for a trial-lawyer husband, overflow patients in a husband's busy medical practice, bookkeeping, office administration, management. A daughter socialized to obey and perform filial obligations may simply transfer her domestic attitudes to an occupational context and may never feel conflict or be considered unfeminine.

The second process is closely allied with the first and overlaps it. It occurs in integrated situations where home and work combine to constitute the female role; it may be the same joint practice involving man and wife or father and daughter; it is not unlike a common pattern in small businesses, where the wife is behind the counter or cash register while the husband buys and does outside selling. Again, the woman has been socialized to be the perfect helpmate and finds her fulfillment of the task in the occupational sphere. Indeed, she would violate the female role if she remained at home while her husband needed her. In both cases, her focus and area of specialty are *his* and are not a projection or reflection of her own talents and propensities.

The factors which enter into the socialization of the young girl, either to a traditional female role or toward a role which includes an orientation towards career, are only the beginning of the story. The following chapters explore the social elements which enhance or impede performance in a career by those who have successfully passed the first hurdles.

III

RECONCILIATION OF WOMEN'S ROLES: PATHS AND OBSTACLES

THE problem of the "many roles" of American women (sociologists use the term "statuses" [1]) has become a cliché even in the popular press. Yet the problems women face in meeting the role demands attached to their many statuses are crucial to their participation in the professional world. The working woman's statuses are acquired both as a result of central female-role-related choices (wife, mother) made during her progress through life, and as a result of her personal choice to work, for example, to become a lawyer or artist. The problems facing a woman who combines the statuses of wife-mother and professional are:

[1] Status is defined as a social position which is institutionalized, like mother, physician. As Goode points out "role" and "status" have often been used interchangeably (in "Norm Commitment and Conformity to Role Status Obligations," *American Journal of Sociology* 66 (November 1960), 246–258). We use the definition as given by Merton in outlining the categories (statuses) but will speak of role strain or role demands as used by Goode ("A Theory of Role Strain," *American Sociological Review*, pp. 483–496).

The combination of statuses a woman holds at any one time — her status set — has consequences for the acquisition of new statuses or the elimination of those she has held.

The female-sex-linked statuses are weighted in respect to the other statuses in a woman's status set.

The role demands attached to any one status may be overdemanding.[2]

The norms governing role behavior are often ambiguous, with resultant discrepancies between expected behavior and expressed attitudes.

There is a lack of consensus on role behavior expected of the woman professional by members of each role set.[3]

There are cultural preferences and expectations about the appropriateness of the specific statuses which may combine to form status sets.

All human beings have an array of statuses which generally reflect and shape their behavior and expectations in life. Furthermore, in all societies certain statuses are found more frequently in certain combinations, as, for example, the grouping which includes wife, mother, and housekeeper.

Women face the problem of being the wrong sex in professional life because there are expectations in society and in the professions about the compatibility of different statuses in status sets.[4] "Status-set typing" occurs when a class of persons shares statuses (that is, certain statuses tend to cluster) *and when it is considered appropriate that they do so*. The upper stratum of the legal profession, for example, is status-set typed because it is commonly expected and preferred that lawyers will share not only their common occupational status (the "functionally

---

[2] Goode, "A Theory of Role Strain," *op. cit.*, p. 485.

[3] *Ibid.*

[4] A status set is defined by Merton as the complement of social statuses of an individual; "Reference Groups and Group Structure" in his *Social Theory and Social Structure*, p. 370. The dynamics of status sets, including the consequences of status sets which occur infrequently and which do not conform to cultural expectations, is a subject which has been dealt with extensively by Professor Merton in lectures at Columbia University over the past few years. This analysis draws upon his conceptualization of many of these questions.

relevant"[5] status conferred by admission to the bar), but other
statuses — for example, white, male, and Anglo-Saxon — some
of which are irrelevant to the practice of law. (The latter statuses are believed to complement the occupational status, although they may not be necessary for performance of the professional task.) The configuration of statuses encountered in
any case of status-set typing is the one found most frequently in
combination. When statuses occur in a combination not typically found, the situation is considered "news" and it makes
people feel uncomfortable. Both of these reactions are illustrated by the way in which the rigid status-set typing of the
British legal profession recently created a Chaplinesque protocol crisis when confronted with the appointment of a woman
judge, Mrs. Elizabeth Lane, to the High Court of Justice. The
Lord Chancellor's Office, charged with resolving the matter,
decreed that, for reasons of protocol, the lady should be referred to as a man. According to *Time* magazine's account of
the crisis and its resolution:

Only four women barristers have yet earned the elite title of
Queen's Counsel (senior barrister). Only one women Q.C. has
yet become a judge in one of Britain's nearly 400 county courts.
Not surprisingly, the elevation of that same woman to the
country's No. 3 tribunal, the High Court of Justice, has touched
off a splendidly British protocol crisis.

Visually, Mrs. Elizabeth Lane, 60, will look little different
from her male colleagues when she dons her gown and wig
and joins four other new appointees as the first woman among
the High Court's 62 justices. But the problem is: what should
lawyers call her. "My Lord" seemed confusing at best, while
traditionalists cringed at the sound of "Mrs. Justice." After
grave deliberation, the Lord Chancellor's office has duly issued
its decision: henceforth, Mrs. Lane will be Mr. Justice Lane,
and may indeed be called "My Lord." "There simply isn't any
precedent for calling a woman anything different," argued a

---

[5] Functionally relevant in Merton's sense of being *task*-linked.

harassed official. "We've taken what seems the least absurd decision."

His Lordship, Mr. Justice Lane, is also entitled by ancient judicial tradition to a bachelor knighthood. . . .[6]

The major consequence of a person's acquisition of a status which "should" not fit in with the others he holds is that irrelevant statuses will be focused upon, or activated. In such deviant cases, the irrelevant status is the *salient* status.[7]

Notions regarding the proper progression from one status to another, the status-sequence,[8] also follow cultural preferences and expectations. The sequence of statuses which culminate in a major status position manifest statistical regularities and are culturally typed. This does not necessarily reflect a sense of moral rightness, but rather a sense of appropriateness about the progression. It is appropriate but not necessarily "just" that John D. Rockefeller II accepts the stewardship of wealth with the ultimate status of "philanthropist" after having gone through a life-style sequence of student at an elite school, husband to a "proper" wife, and businessman in a great corporation. It has always been easier for the well-to-do boy to proceed from Groton to Harvard to Harvard Law School and from there to a "Wall Street" law practice,[9] than for the poor boy who went to public primary and high schools and the College of the City of New York to attain that professional position. It would be unlikely that the poor boy, no matter what his ability, would accumulate a status set (member of the N. Y. Athletic Club, Social Register listee, Republican committeeman, etc.) seen as harmonious with the high occupational status of Wall Street lawyer.

One status supports another; one can get richer having rich associates who enable one to meet important people easily and

[6] *Time* (August 27, 1965), p. 40.
[7] This follows Merton's definition of salience in his analysis of the dynamics of status sets (definitions from unpublished lectures).
[8] Defined by Merton as "the succession of statuses occurring with sufficient frequency as to be socially patterned"; *Social Theory and Social Structure*, p. 370.
[9] Discussed in Smigel, *The Wall Street Lawyer*.

have access to information and resources. Although one can fail despite having an easy route, it is easier to succeed. Of course there are exceptions. Poor boys can become rich, and women can become professors of physics, but these achievements are considered noteworthy as oddities. The patterned route as well as the patterned complex of statuses seems correct and does not need explanation.

There are limits to the range of variations possible in the status sequence and the status set.[10] A man with a blue-collar job and eight children is not likely to become a candidate for high political office. There is a good chance that he has little education, belongs to a sect religion or is Catholic, the sum of which reduces his chances for high political office. Similarly, a woman with eight children and a husband who believes that woman's place is in the home has a slim chance of practicing law *even* if she has a law degree. Not because any one status (father or mother of eight, or Catholic, or wife) is itself a total deterrent to high political office, or to the practice of law, but because the totality of the demands and hardships to be surmounted are such that one's inner resources and social exposure are statistically more likely to be insufficient.

When statuses and roles are interwoven they comprise institutions, and institutions may not be integrated with each other; thus, the family system may place strains on the economic or the political or the religious sphere. If one cluster of statuses seems supportive of a structure (for example, if the staff members of a prestigious teaching hospital also share the statuses of Harvard Medical School graduate, Presbyterian, son of professional father, Westchester home owner) we should examine the case carefully and assess the cost to the rest of society.[11]

A too inclusive clustering of statuses indicates that the team

---

[10] Barriers against combining various roles are discussed in Goode's "A Theory of Role Strain," *op. cit.*, p. 491.

[11] See E. Digby Baltzell's "Caste and the Corporation," chapter 14 in *The Protestant Establishment* (New York: Random House, 1964), for his perceptive tracing of the consequences of status-set typing in American industry (although he does not identify it as such).

which results probably works well together, but that it constitutes an impenetrable in-group. The status set which seems so harmonious effectively bars other segments of society. And if many of society's elite status sets bar specific subgroups — for example, Negroes — the result will be reinforcement of the kind of cultural determinism that defines low-ranking service and labor jobs as socially and culturally appropriate for them.[12] The process of cultural determinism probably is even more effective in assigning women to particular spheres of the labor market.

Introduce a woman into the club of senators and immediately the Senate "establishment" has suffered a blow. The work of all-night discussions in private clubs, man-to-man talks, and political deals over a drink are exclusive of the society of women in our culture. I recall reading an anecdote related by Perle Mesta about an embarrassing incident that arose when a woman senator was a guest at a diplomatic dinner party. When the men withdrew for brandy and political talk after dinner and the woman gathered in another room for coffee and women's talk, the question arose as to which group the lady senator should join. Miss Mesta reports that the lady herself chose to go with the men; quite appropriately, judged the hostess.

Perhaps if half the Senate seats were filled by women instead of only one or two this division across sex lines might never arise. Hostesses would guide all their guests to coffee and brandy in the same room, and those who wished to talk politics could find one another while those who chose to talk about servant problems or baseball could gravitate toward each other. There can be no doubt that the status of "man" and the status of "high political officer" have been drawn as compatible and thereby natural and right. This points up a basic sociological dictum: To the extent that a status is institutionalized within a

[12] This is another dimension of the self-fulfilling prophecy as outlined by Merton in "The Self-Fulfilling Prophecy," chapter 11 in *Social Theory and Social Structure*, p. 436.

body of other statuses and there are definite prescriptions as to the total composition, and to the extent to which one social pattern (social circle and social customs) is integrated with another social pattern (occupation and mode of operation within the occupation), the range of other possible combinations of statuses will be limited. If the Senate must also be a club and its members must be homogenous, then the unclubbable Senator must find it difficult to work effectively within it, be that Senator a maverick, a Buddhist, a midget, or a woman.

Acquiring Statuses

Robert Merton has pointed out that some statuses are more "dominant" than others in that they may limit or facilitate the acquisition of other statuses. For example, if I know that someone is a middle-class woman, I can feel safe in predicting that she does *not* also hold the status of corporation manager. The salient status in a status set is the one activated by the individual and his role partners and becomes the object of focus in interaction. The salient status may be the irrelevant one (often because it is not normally found in combination with the other statuses with which it appears) in any given context. (If we are at a business meeting and the lady has indeed turned out to be a corporation manager, I will be most conscious of the fact that she is a woman even though I ought to keep my mind on whether she is a good "businessman" or not.) The salient status then may draw the attention of the members of one's various role sets to the exclusion of other statuses which may be more relevant. Certain ascribed statuses — sex status and racial status, for example — are central in controlling the choices of most individuals. The status of "woman" is one such dominant and often salient status. For a woman, sex status is primary and pivotal and it inevitably determines much of the course of her life, especially because of rigid cultural definitions which limit the range of other statuses she may acquire. (There is also a culturally fixed constellation for men. Goffman, for example, has pointed out that even the American male's status set should conform to the preferred pattern and, to the extent that one's status set falls short of the valued image, there are likely to be upsetting consequences for behavior.[13])

In addition to her sex status of female, the woman's other statuses are usually linked closely; she is a wife and a mother, a daughter and perhaps a sister; although she may become a physician or engineer, this is not likely. If she does acquire a professional status then it is likely that her sex status will become salient in the professional context, and her professional status may become salient in her family life. Around each of the female-associated statuses a woman acquires revolves a complex network of roles that is likely to increase in demand as class rank rises and to prove a formidable problem to the middle-class woman seeking to acquire or maintain a professional status.

The professional woman probably has fewer mechanisms than the man for coping with the expectations of the over-demanding role networks revolving around her sex-linked and occupational statuses, even if it is assumed that nearly everyone must cope with an overtaxing set of role demands and that consensus exists about appropriate behavior in any specific role. Under certain circumstances, of course, an individual woman may find that her statuses are congruent and that her role partners are not pulling her in all directions. Such a woman is fortunate. There are women too, who do not rely on destiny, but who work to make their status sets congruent and who utilize a number of mechanisms, which we describe later, to make their lives easier — even when their lives are essentially non-conformist and they buck the tide of typical expectations.

[13] "In an important sense there is only one complete unblushing male in America: a young, married, white, urban, northern, heterosexual Protestant father of college education, fully employed, of good complexion, weight, height, and a recent record in sports. Every American male tends to look out upon the world from this perspective, this constituting one sense in which one can speak of a common value system in America. Any male who fails to qualify in any of these ways is likely to view himself — during moments at least — as unworthy, incomplete and inferior. . . ." Goffman, *Stigma: Notes on the Management of Spoiled Identity*, p. 128.

MARRIAGE AND PROFESSIONAL LIFE

One status almost all American women are apt to acquire is that of wife. My study of women lawyers and the studies of women in other professions [14] suggest that even women in professional positions now are more likely to be married than in the past and that more married women are rising to positions of prestige within the professions. A generation ago women often chose between marriage and a career, or, at least, these were seen as the principal alternatives. Career women in the past most often have been spinsters, divorcees, or widows. In 1940, two-thirds of all professional women were single; 8 percent were widowed or divorced.[15] This was in an era when a sizable proportion of women remained spinsters. But there have been changes. First, not only is the label "spinster" becoming a relic (the "bachelor girl" has replaced her), but the status itself is becoming passé. The percentage of unmarried American woman in their early thirties decreased to 7 percent in 1963, from 15 percent in 1960,[16] and the proportion of women who will never marry has been projected to only 3 percent by the time the generation of women who were in their late twenties and early thirties in the mid-1960's enters middle age. Although the percentage of women remaining single might easily increase a bit,[17] the choice for career in place of marriage is probably no longer a consideration of young women. The new decision is for marriage alone, or marriage with career.

A few years ago, the decision for marriage, precluding career, was made more conclusive by the steady lessening of the

[14] Alice Rossi's, for example. See "Barriers to the Career Choice of Engineering, Medicine or Science Among American Women," p. 74.

[15] Marguerite Zapoleon, "College Women and Employment," in Opal D. David (ed.), *The Education of Women*, p. 57.

[16] "Spinsters' Ratio Declining in U.S.," *New York Times* (June 3, 1963), p. 31.

[17] There is some evidence that there is a decreasing ratio of males to females in the prime ages of marriage. But the sex ratio is expected to normalize at a slightly higher number of males to females in the 1970's. See Jeanne Clare Ridley, "Demographic Change and the Roles and Status of Women," *The Annals of the American Academy of Political and Social Science* 375 (January 1968), 15–25.

age of marriage of Americans, 20.3 for women in 1961. Even women college graduates marry early, their most frequent age at marriage being 22. Although Americans seem to be waiting a little longer to marry today, their typical age at marriage is still the lowest in the Western World. Early marriage has meant early motherhood and, during the years of the great baby boom, 1946–1957, more motherhood. Of course the consequences of this were less time and fewer resources to devote to advanced training, a pattern that had deleterious effects on women's participation in the professions. Jessie Bernard has shown the inverse relationship between the fertility rate and the proportion of advanced degrees earned by women during the baby-boom decade — a period she has called the interlude of "motherhood mania." [18] It is not that fewer women work as a result of marriage and children, but that fewer have career-type jobs. In 1920 the average woman worker was single and 28 years of age. Today the average woman worker is married and 41 years of age. Most have returned to the job market after their children have grown, although one-third of working women have children under 18. Over the past two decades there has been an enormous rise in the number of women working outside the home. Not only are more women in the labor force now than ever before, but the majority status among them has shifted to the married group. Married women have increased their participation in the labor force from one out of every five married (in 1947) to one out of three (in 1967). Nearly 60 percent of all working women are married as contrasted with about 40 percent twenty years ago.[19]

In 1968 more than half of the female labor force were married women. But these married women tend to be found in the lower ranks of the occupational hierarchy.

What about women at the top? Is this group different?

[18] Bernard, "The Status of Women in Modern Patterns of Culture," *Annals of the American Academy of Political and Social Science* 375 (January 1968), 9.
[19] Citizen's Advisory Council on the Status of Women, "Report of the Task Force on Labor Standards to the Citizen's Advisory Council on the Status of Women," (Washington, D.C.: U.S. Government Printing Office, 1968), p. 6.

Some studies have shown that, among those who rose to the top of their profession, the incidence of unmarried women was greater. For example, two-thirds of the top women in federal civil service posts were unmarried.[20] Havemann and West's study of a sample of college students [21] showed that a great majority of the career women never married, a fairly substantial minority were widows, and a few were divorcees. A far higher percentage of the unmarried, compared to men, tend to be found in the ranks of the professions. Even in 1960, those women employed in the scientific and engineering fields were considerably less likely to be married than men — two out of five women scientists as contrasted with four out of five men.[22] Similar percentages are true for women in other male-dominated professions as Table 7 indicates.

Because far fewer single women are available to fill the reservoir of potential career women that existed in the past, if women are even to maintain their hold on, much less increase, their participation in professional work they will have to combine the statuses of wife and professional worker.

Single women face fewer structural problems in handling the demands of a career since they have no obligations as wives and mothers. But married women do, of course. Therefore, the presence of large numbers of married women in the work force has led to institutional and cultural disharmony. Although there have been changes in the composition of the female work force there have been few deep changes in social attitudes toward married working women, especially toward those who may be said to have careers.

In fact, women who today choose both marriage and a career

[20] U.S. Civil Service Commission Statistics Section, *Study of Employment of Women in the Federal Government, 1967* (Washington, D.C.: U.S. Government Printing Office, June 1968), p. 3.

[21] Havemann and West, *They Went to College: The College Graduate in America Today*, pp. 76–77.

[22] Rossi, "Barriers to the Career Choice of Engineering, Medicine or Science Among American Women," *op. cit.*, pp. 72–78. Also see Bernard's data on marriage among professional women in chapter 14, "Spinsters," of her *Academic Women*, and in the footnotes to that chapter.

TABLE 8

Marital Status of Lawyers, Scientists, Engineers, and Physicians, by Sex
(Percentage of experienced civilian labor force, U.S., 1960)

Occupation		Single	Married, spouse present	Separated, divorced, widowed	Widowed	Divorced	Base number
Law	Men	8.2	86.8	4.9	1.9	1.8	202,341
	Women	32.2	45.6	22.1	9.2	9.6	7,343
Scientists, natural	Men	13.0	84.0	3.0			135,649
	Women	45.0	43.0	12.0			14,616
Engineers	Men	9.0	88.0	2.0			862,002
	Women	37.0	45.0	18.0			7,714
Physicians and surgeons	Men	7.0	88.0	5.0	2.1	1.1	214,830
	Women	31.0	51.0	18.0	7.0	7.0	15,477
Professors-Instructors:							
Natural scientists[a]	Men	17.0	79.0	4.0			31,474
	Women	56.0	33.0	11.0			3,911
Engineering	Men	12.0	86.0	2.0			9,805
	Women	36.0	64.0	—			221

Source: U.S. Bureau of the Census, Census of Population, 1960. Subject Reports. *Occupational Characteristics*, Final Report PC (2)-7A, 1963, Table 12.
[a] Includes agricultural sciences, biological sciences, chemistry, geology, mathematics, physics, and natural sciences not otherwise classified.

face a nearly normless situation in that no formal structure or
expectations exist to aid them in apportioning time and resources between their two major responsibilities. Ability to deal
with the complex roles of wife, mother, working woman, especially at the professional level, is still largely a matter of individual adaptation, compromise, and personal arrangement,
often characterized by strain. Although fewer women professionals are spinsters, those who marry have a good chance of di-
vorcing. The proportion of divorced professional women is substantially higher than that of professional men.

Hierarchy in the Status Set

Why must the woman who aspires to a professional career be
a nonconformist? Why have so many been single? What barriers has society stacked against her? Most fundamentally, the
woman professional must face a conflict in the hierarchy of status priorities in Western society. For women, the obligations attached to family statuses are first in priority, while for men the
role demands deriving from the occupational status ordinarily
override all others. The woman's duties as a mother override
most other role obligations, her duties as a wife are second, and
other status obligations are usually a poor third.

The woman who acquires the status of professional acquires
with it a seemingly insurmountable problem of role strain:
Should she conform to the demands imposed on her because
she is a mother or wife, or should she give priority to those demands which come as a result of being a doctor or scientist?
What must she do when, as often occurs, the two conflict?

The role strain experienced by the woman professional can
easily become constant and enervating, aggravated by the ambiguity that makes necessary a new decision for each minor conflict, and by the often conflicting positions taken by other people in her role network.

The man is to a great extent shielded from conflict "by the
existence in his environment of a hierarchy of values which pre-
clude, for the most part, the necessity of conscious decision. Un-

less family needs reach crisis proportion, the demands of his work come first. And neither he nor his wife is faced with problems of choice in a condition of crisis." [23]

Persons engaged in professional activity are especially expected to channel a large proportion of their emotional and physical energies into work. Not only is achievement a positive good, but in the tradition of the Protestant ethic, work itself is good and often its own excuse. The man who spends too much time with his family is considered something of a loafer.

Furthermore, a man's duties and obligations *as a husband* fall primarily in the occupational sphere. If he earns an adequate living for his family, he has nearly fulfilled society's demands on him and, depending on his social rank, he has a wide range of acceptable behavior within which he may fulfill his other husband-father roles. For example, he is admired if he likes to putter around the house, but if he can afford it he can pay a handyman to do home repairs with little loss of esteem. If he likes sports he can play ball with his son, but if he prefers sedentary activities no one will hold it against him if he instead plays chess or checkers or builds model airplanes with his child. He must, of course, show some interest in his child to be considered a good father in our society, but a little is often enough. It is not even as onerous to be labeled a poor father as it is to be called a poor mother. Expectations about what is an adequate amount of time for a man to be with his wife are also imprecise; a man's other activities, starting with work obligations but including clubs, hobbies, politics, and informal male social get-togethers, all are legitimate reasons for cutting down on this time. Assuming that the husband is not spending time away from home to be with another woman, the wife is given little legitimation for objecting to his absence. The wife who does object and who demands that her husband remain home is likely to be labeled a "nag." In addition, the husband may feel free to be away from home and family, knowing that his wife

[23] Lotte Bailyn, "Notes on the Role of Choice in the Psychology of Professional Women," pp. 706–707.

is there to take care of things, to supervise the children's activities, to manage the house. In extreme cases of neglect, wives
may be permitted to complain, but clearly the absorption of the
man in his work is not considered intolerable. Professors who
prefer their work to their wives or children are usually "understood" and forgiven.[24] A similar absorption in work was reported by Stanley Talbot in *Time* magazine; he found that the
business tycoon (not surprisingly) clearly preferred his work to
his family.[25] There is no comparable "lady tycoon" with a husband and children to neglect; and the lady professional who
gives any indication of being more absorbed in work than in
her husband and family is neither understood nor forgiven.
The woman, unlike the man, cannot spend "too much time"
with her family; her role demands as mother and wife are such
that they intrude on all other activities. She remains on call
during any time spent away from the family and, if she works,
many of her family tasks must be fitted into what usually
would be working time.[26]

Since the woman who works must deal with two conflicting
priority systems (occupational demands are not lowered for the
woman though she may consider them second in importance),
she may often find herself under strain to perform both roles
adequately.

It is often assumed that a woman's professional commitments
deflect her from home obligations and vice versa. A man may
find that being a husband supports his occupational roles.[27]
Edwin Boring and Alice Bryan have observed, in a study of
factors affecting the professional careers of women psychologists, that "Women averaged 14.1 hours per week on familial
or domestic activities as compared with 10.6 hours for the men.

[24] See Jessie Bernard's comments in "Wives and Mothers," chapter 15 of
Academic Women, pp. 215–241.
[25] *Time* (November 10, 1952), p. 109.
[26] Bryan and Boring, "Women in American Psychology: Factors Affecting
Their Professional Careers," *American Psychologist* 2 (January 1947), 3–20.
[27] See Goode's analysis of the interlocking of role obligations, "A Theory of
Role Strain," *op. cit.*, p. 491.

Three or more hours per week were spent on child-training and guidance by 29.4 percent of women, on physical care of children by 24.5 percent, and on special problems of children by 10.2 percent." [28]

In a later study, Boring also noted that nearly all the male psychologists are married, and "a married man usually manages to make his marriage contribute to his success and prestige. Most of the married women do not receive the same professional support from their husbands and the unmarried women have no husbands." [29] Riesman has pointed to the married male professor's advantage in having a wife, "who even if she does pursue a part-time career, guards her husband's productivity and performance in obvious and in subtle ways, just as her husband's secretary or the woman librarian . . . speeds him on his way." [30] The man's status set is complementary and reinforcing and the woman's is not. The professional woman who marries and permits proliferation of her family statuses must early face the fact that she has no wife at home.

Family Roles

What are the role demands on the wife which lead to conflict with her possible or actual occupational roles?

To begin with, the American conjugal family system heavily weights the obligations of the woman's roles in the family — far beyond those of the man. The obligations of the mother-wife role are rigorously demanding of the woman. Indeed, they have typically constituted a full-time occupation in spite of the observations of Talcott Parsons [31] and other sociologists who claim that the American woman has little to do. Although many share his view that the "utilitarian aspect of the role of the housewife . . . has declined in importance to the point

---

[28] Bryan and Boring, *op. cit.*, pp. 17–18.
[29] Boring, "The Woman Problem," p. 681.
[30] David Riesman, in his introduction to Jessie Bernard, *Academic Women*, p. xxiv.
[31] In "Age and Sex in the Social Structure of the United States," pp. 89–103.

where it scarcely approaches a full-time occupation for a vigorous person,"[32] it is obvious to all that most middle-class women do fill their days in a myriad of household activities.

Unlike the extended family, in which a division of household labor is possible among numbers of kin, in the conjugal family the primary responsibility for managing the household falls to the wife. Even though some paid domestic help often is feasible, she must administer the household and as a manager is responsible for a very large number of tasks. These responsibilities become more numerous with income, class position, and number of children. They also seem to proliferate in middle age. Whether or not all these tasks are essential or could be eliminated does not mitigate the fact that they demand decision and are usually not easy to delegate to others.

Note, too, that the burden of these tasks is nearly constant and repetitive; food must be planned daily, children's activities occur throughout each day, and in the evening the husband wants and expects his wife to be a good companion or just to "be around." In clear conflict with this schedule, which demands that the wife be "on tap" from time to time, are the needs of the professional for large blocks of uninterrupted time. Snatches of time taken here and there are not additive,[33] and snatches of time are often all that the housewife can muster.

It is, perhaps, worthwhile to compare the house-tending duties of American women with those of housewives in a country where things are not as "easy," for American women have more and better mechanical housekeeping aids than women in any other society.

Much has been said about labor-saving devices freeing women from household tasks to do more productive or pleasurable things. At a conference on the Role and Status of Women

[32] *Ibid.*, p. 98.
[33] Bailyn, *op. cit.*, p. 706. Goode, too, has commented on the great amount of administrative work handled by the women, also suggesting that this capacity could be tapped for managerial work in business and the professions.

in Soviet Russia held a few years ago,[34] it was often pointed out by participating American social scientists and corroborated by Soviet women panelists that the lack of labor-saving devices in Russian households posed many difficulties for women. Most Soviet women, they reported, had two occupations — an outside job or career and a housekeeping job. The housekeeping job was unrelieved by either domestic help or the household appliances commonly taken for granted in the United States, such as vacuum cleaners and refrigerators. Like other European men, and unlike Americans, Soviet husbands typically do not, and are not expected to, help in the household. Mark Field, a Soviet studies specialist, observed that Russian women spent up to three hours daily tending to their households in addition to whatever time they spent at their paid jobs. The long work day of Soviet women has also been attested to by *New York Times* correspondent Elena Whiteside, from observations made while on a visit to members of her family in the Soviet Union.[35] She noted that it was typical for them to spend six hours a day in homemaking after seven hours on the job (including a half-day on Saturday). In addition to the housekeeping tasks known to American women, the Soviet wife's six hours of homemaking included marketing every day (essential because of the lack of refrigerators) and hand washing of laundry (including diapers and the endless changes of clothing required by young children). Whiteside emphasized the pressure on the Soviet housewife to complete all housework as early as possible because apartments were small and overcrowded; kitchen tables had to do double duty as desks for children's homework, and perhaps the homework of spouses and of parents who might share the apartment.[36]

In comparison to the household situation of Soviet women and women in other eastern and even western European coun-

[34] At Bryn Mawr College, Bryn Mawr, Pa., April 23, 1964.

[35] Elena Whiteside, "For Soviet Women: A Thirteen-Hour Day," pp. 28 *ff.*

[36] Study is stressed in the Soviet Union and observers report that it is common for working people to take courses.

tries, American women are most royally endowed in the quantity, quality, and extensiveness of labor-saving devices in the home. Machines wash and dry dishes, wash floors and rugs; special preparations are available to make dusting and waxing simple and effective; cloth is treated to reject soiling and staining. Food is easily available, packaged to meet requirements of all sizes of families, to suit gourmet tastes as well as to provide simple fare; thanks to spacious refrigerators, food purchasing can be accomplished in a few hours once or twice a week. American women are not dependent on the weather or the calendar to wash, clean, or purchase; they do not have to wait on line to buy scarce items on their shopping lists. Even the Russians concede that American women live under more favorable conditions for housekeeping than they do.[37]

This may present a paradox. With labor-saving devices, freedom of choice and movement in scheduling her activities, and the heralded and disputed participation of American husbands in the care and management of the home, women in the United States prefer not to leave the world of the home for the world of socially defined productive (that is, paid) labor, whereas Soviet women, without help and without conveniences, manage to do two jobs.

Apparently the burden of housekeeping is not the prime deterrent, since those American working-class women who must work and those American women who choose to work — among them the 6 percent of doctors and 3 percent of lawyers who are women — manage to find solutions to the problem.

It would not be accurate to paint a portrait of an indolent class of American women who sit idly by while robot hands do their unbidden tasks; the work day of the American woman is quite as long as that of most other women of the world. The American woman is, rather, subject to Northcote Parkinson's law that "work expands to fill the time allotted for it." As

[37] In 1956, Premier Khrushchev (at the 20th Party Congress) urged the need for his country to develop labor-saving devices and prepared foods to ease the burdens of the Soviet woman.

cleaning aids have been improved, standards of cleanliness have been upgraded far beyond the thresholds of sanitation necessary for health. With the new easy-to-use machinery, many jobs once relegated to others outside the home have returned to the home: the carpets which were sent out once a year to be cleaned or were beaten over the clotheslines in the spring now are washed every month with a machine devised expressly for that purpose; laundry often is washed daily because of the availability of washing machines and dryers, and this has made it possible for everyone to have a change of clothing, bedding, and linen more frequently. The list is endless and oppressive to the housewife. American women have engrossed themselves in housework and made their homes their career.

Can't Surrogates Do It?

The compulsion of the American housewife is to have her home clean and her children safe and happy, but the question is: Must she do the whole job herself? There is probably considerable psychological variance in the need of individual women to achieve these goals themselves. Theoretically, at least, some of them could delegate some of these tasks to others. If the middle-class woman hopes to use her education and to work productively, alternative means of performing the household functions of the wife-mother must be sought. Here, however, the "freedom" of the woman to choose what she would like to do may also be theoretical. There are few institutional arrangements on which anyone can really rely (day-care centers for children, bonded housekeepers, and the like): in addition, few norms exist to govern and legitimize their use. Furthermore, the woman cannot turn to her husband automatically to fill in for her. If a woman's profession requires that she travel occasionally or attend meetings, or if she should simply wish to attend social get-togethers that might bring in clients or help her air work problems, she must herself make arrangements for the home to run smoothly in her absence. Probably only rarely can a woman depend on her husband for the same kind of overall supervision of house and children that the husband can be sure of when his wife is home.

The Further Complications of Early Marriage

As we noted before, American women, even college graduates, marry very early. What is the effect of early marriage on the decision to combine marriage with a career?

If a young woman decides to marry early she has put herself in a position where she has taken on many more role demands than she anticipated acquiring and which compete heavily with the demands of career preparation. Not only does she have a husband, but she has added a set of relationships with his family and friends. In becoming a wife, she has also become the target of pressures and expectations regarding her behavior. Her new world may often clash with her world of work or education. The entire character of her interaction with friends may change, and her energies may have to be redirected to the establishment of a home and the service of her husband's career rather than her own.

It is no doubt true that where priorities must be established about whose career must give way it is the female's, whether it is allocation of the family budget when the student wife starts to work to support the graduate studies of the husband, or the choice of locality for maximizing the career possibilities of the husband without considering the training or work possibilities of the wife. This is not to say that husbands do not in fact forsake opportunities for advancement if it means moving somewhere where the wife will not be happy or, if the wife is an established professional, where she has no opportunity to set up practice. But there is in this society no norm prescribing that the decision must include the weighting of the wife's needs as a consideration. A young woman is not likely to work out in advance with a prospective husband an arrangement for living which includes her work requirements. In a dispute over choice of locality in which to settle, for instance, her ties to her family might provide a more legitimate reason than her job plans.

For instance, a man rarely need concern himself with the demands of his wife's time schedule or her interests in arranging his own work schedule. It is assumed she will mold her schedule to fit his if necessary and even sacrifice such attachments as locale or friendships if the husband's job requires that he relocate. If he is required to work late or work weekends, the wife is expected to take over all household demands and obligations. At the very least he can depend on society to legitimate his behavior; the wife who complains excessively is considered selfish or nagging. The assumption is that the family benefits from his activity provided such disruptions are not constant. Even then, the leeway is broad and the full dedication of a man to work allows little room for legitimate complaint from wife or family.

We might assume that if a woman marries after she has become a professional the problems of husband's negative attitudes is diminished; she has already chosen and need not wait for his approval. But for the young girl just deciding whether or not to work, the image of a potentially disapproving husband may well intimidate; if she marries young, she will accept the culturally established priority of her husband's training before hers. In the Ross study of top Michigan students, of those who married as undergraduates, it was found that "the attitudes of the husband and of the husband's family made it necessary for peace and harmony that the young wife adjust to conventional, traditional and conforming ways."[38] The young girl no longer participated in "the dynamic interaction between herself and the university culture" — the sororities or student organizations.

Early marriage, in addition, is likely to result in early childbearing, a further impediment to the work decision. Not only is the woman who marries early and has children early less likely to work at all but, even if she has had some specialized training, she has fewer structural supports for its use. She is probably in a lower economic bracket than the later-marrying,

[38] Ross, *op. cit.*, p. 76.

later-childbearing woman; she is probably less experienced and has fewer professional contacts to help her get high-level positions, so that the difference between her earned income and what she must pay out for child care is considerably smaller than it is for the woman who is advanced in her professional work.

Children

There have been changes in the definition of children's roles and mothers' roles which create intense demands on the American woman. Children's roles have changed so that offspring are dependent on the family longer; at least the family feels responsible for its youth longer. Even though families are now smaller, many child-caring activities have been prolonged. The middle-class mother has recently been so sensitized to her role in the development of the child that she is always conscious of the consequences of her habits, techniques, and emotions — making the mother-child relationship pervading and depleting her energies.[39] Although the presence of the mother in the home is widely touted as important, many children in their teens (and even before) seem to be running from their ever-scrutinizing mamas.

But mothers have not been freed from the cultural mandate to know and see all about their children. It is not considered proper for children to be raised by anyone other than the mother. Grandparents may baby-sit, but it is recognized that this is to relieve the mother at her main task, not to free her for other obligations. Of course, many grandmothers do act as surrogate mothers for their grandchildren while their daughters work, but this pattern is informal and not normative. This is not to say that it is infrequent. Yudkin and Holme found in an English study of working mothers that one-third of their pre-

---

[39] Although there have been many studies of socialization patterns of middle-class and lower-class parents, the focus has usually been on the effect on the child. I suggest that an interesting and important area of research would be the study of the effect of socialization to parental roles (generally and by class) on parents.

school children were looked after by grandmothers.[40] And in the symposium on Soviet Woman cited above, Soviet women exchange students noted that in their country it was common for grandmothers to care for children.[41] In the United States, working mothers who have children under 12 have them cared for principally by a member of the family. Although a survey of child-care arrangements of working mothers distinguished only between fathers and "other relatives" we suppose that this latter category is largely made up of grandmothers; it constituted 21 percent of child-care arrangements made. Fathers constituted 15 percent. Together, arrangements by members of the family added to 45 percent (including relatives other than the grandmother) and was the most frequent type of child care.[42] Only 10 percent of children under 14 are cared for by maids, baby-sitters, or housekeepers in the United States and only 2 percent are in group care, such as day-care centers, nursery schools, and after-school centers.[43] Since 1962 some additional provisions have been made for day-care services, but they remain grossly inadequate to the need and middle-class women rarely use them. Dodge reports that a wider range of child-care facilities exists in the Soviet Union but there, too, they are not adequate to the need. Perhaps only in the Scandinavian countries have attractive surrogate child-care facilities been provided for the general public. The problem is further complicated for American women by the fact that popular child-care authorities have reinforced the norms specifying that mothers should stay home with their young children. Dr. Benjamin Spock and Dr. Bruno Bettelheim, both in books and in their advice columns in popular women's magazines, urge mothers to forsake employment during the child's early years. Thus the mothers

[40] Yudkin and Holme, *Working Mothers and Their Children*, p. 54.
[41] This is corroborated in Norton T. Dodge, *Women in the Soviet Economy*, p. 28.
[42] Seth Low and Pearl G. Spindler, *Child Care Arrangements of Working Mothers in the United States* (Washington, D.C.: U.S. Government Printing Office, 1968), Children's Bureau Publication number 461, p. 15.
[43] *Ibid.*, p. 16.

not only have difficulty finding good care for their children, they also feel guilty about it. In the socialist countries, women may have difficulty finding good care for their children also, but they do not face cultural condemnation.

Another — and a major — set of demands is made on the mother by the extended role network into which she is inevitably drawn as her child grows. This network includes other parents and institutional structures which operate on the assumption that the mothers do not work and are therefore always available. Doctors expect mothers, not nurses, to bring children for checkups; many parent-teacher meetings are held during the day (especially for nursery school and play groups). Arrangements for children to visit one another's homes usually result from daytime neighborhood acquaintanceships formed by mothers, and problems will result unless all the mothers in a group work or special arrangements are made for babysitters or nurses to escort children to each other's homes.

The child whose mother is not free to form daytime acquaintanceships with other mothers may be deprived of the companionship of other children except in formal settings. The nonworking mother may feel affronted if the working mother's child comes to visit accompanied by a nurse; the nurse has a lower status than the mother and the children place the two women in a situation which is difficult for informal social interaction. The nonworking mother may discourage this unrewarding situation in favor of the familiar equal-rank relationship with another woman who stays home. There is no problem if both mothers work and the contact is made between nurses, or if the nurse merely brings the child to the nonworking mother's home and leaves him, or if the working mother can arrange for a grandmother to go with the child.

The latter arrangements deprive the mother of control over both the selection of her children's playmates (if the nurses initiate the friendship) and the conditions of the contact, and also deprive her of information about her children's play behavior, their emotional outlook, and so on. Thus, she is often dependent on the observations and evaluations of others (nursery school teachers, for example), whose perceptive equipment may be quite different from the mother's. This may constitute a problem for the contemporary American mother, who has been supersensitized to the psychic needs of early childhood. The problem for the working mother is perhaps worse in the pre-school and early school years when the focus is on the mother-child relationship and the mother is made to bear full responsibility for setting her child's inner psyche and outer environment. As children grow older, the mother's problems may be fewer, not because children's needs are less, but because the focus for much of the child's training shifts from mother to school.

In addition to the problems of care, social contact, and adjustment, there are the usual crises of childhood, most commonly those caused by illness. When the child is ill, his dependency on the mother is more strongly exhibited and the mother's own guilt feelings about leaving the child are strongest. Few mothers can find legitimation in their social environment for leaving a child while he is ill, and few childhood illnesses seem less than severe when one's own child has them; measles, chicken pox, and tonsillitis, with their raging fevers and uncomfortable rashes, are frightening. But people vary in their ability to tolerate the illnesses of those emotionally close to them, and there are also subcultural differences in attitudes toward illness.[44] The mother who has no experience with childhood illnesses and who strongly empathizes with illness doubtless will feel more torn about leaving a sick child than one who believes that childhood diseases are routine if uncomfortable. At such times, the woman's ability to function as a responsible worker (if indeed she does not leave work altogether) as well as a mother will depend on whether she has a confluence of really reliable help, whether the child feels secure with the surrogate caretaker, the extent of the guilt she feels at leaving her

[44] See, for example, Mark Zborowski, "Cultural Components in Response to Pain," *Journal of Social Issues* 18 (1952), 16–30.

child, and the work demands she faces at the moment. If she is lucky, her work schedule will permit her to defer most tasks should a genuine emergency arise. She is luckier if she has children who have few illnesses.

The Family — Its Demands as a Unit

The modern conjugal family has been defined as the emotional-control task center of the society. Goode has identified the sources and the consequences:

The modern technological system is psychologically burdensome on the individual because it demands an unremitting discipline. To the extent that evaluation is based on achievement and universalism, the individual gets little emotional security from his work. . . . Lower level jobs give little pleasure to most people. However, in higher level professional, managerial and creative positions the standards of performance are not only high but are often without clearly stated limits. The individual is under considerable pressure to perform better than he is able.

The conjugal family . . . integrates with such a system by its emphasis on emotionality, especially in the relationship of husband and wife. It has the task of restoring the input-output emotional balance of individualism in such a job structure. This is so even for lower strata jobs where the demand for performance is kept within limits by an understood quota, but where, by contrast with upper-strata jobs, there is less intrinsic job satisfaction.[45]

Although the family unit is seen here as performing the tension-management function, actually it is the job of the woman, the wife and mother, to provide the safety valve that the family's members require for revitalization in their occupations. It is often asserted that if the woman were as deeply involved as the man in an occupation, the system would come under additional strain and the family would suffer. It has historically been the

[45] Goode, *World Revolution and Family Patterns*, p. 14.

job of the woman to soothe the harried breadwinner, although we all know of cases in which the stay-at-home wife creates such tension in the home that the husband flees to the occupational world for a dose of tension management.

SEX-DIVISION OF LABOR IN THE FAMILY

There is a less rigid sex division of labor within the American family than within the European family, and American husbands are said to share in the work of the household; but this has not brought any considerable change in the American woman's basic roles. It is hard to know where the differences lie in the wife-help patterns of American and European men. Here image, attitudes, and behavior may be highly incongruent. American men probably do help their wives more in the absence of the highly structured images of "woman's place" found in Europe, and in the absence, too, of servants in middle-class American households. These factors probably mean that the American male's roles have expanded somewhat in comparison with the European's.[46] The sharing of household duties may lighten the woman's burden, but the help pattern does not give her free time in a form that can be effectively used for professional work.

On the other hand, American women's roles often include tasks which are extensions of their husband's occupational roles. Women may become informal and thus unpaid but necessary members of a work team. Like the ambassador's wife, the corporation executive's wife must socialize, become knowledgeable about the work world of her husband, and operate within its prescribed patterns. Margaret Helfrich has outlined the basic duties and norms of the executive's wife:

(1) To care for the home, husband and children.
(2) To manage so that the husband gets a portion of the wife's time.

[46] See *ibid.*, chapter 2, for a further discussion on this point.

(3) To entertain his business associates and their mutual friends.

(4) To participate in social and civic affairs.

The norms of conduct include: tact, sociability, adaptability, patience and understanding, reserve, intelligence, a sense of humor, and good physical and mental health.[47]

We take little notice of unpaid middle-class working women in the United States. The clamorous voices which challenge the inequities in American life are silent when it comes to the large-scale exploitation of women at the sides of their husbands. Women's work is very visible but no one takes notice of it. Why, for example, is the wife of the President of the United States not given a salary for her around-the-clock attention to affairs of state? The nation's first hostess is responsible for diplomatic receptions at which decisions affecting the entire country may be at stake. Perhaps this job might even be separated from the presidency; after all, not all presidential spouses are equally suited for this demanding work. The nation's First Lady might better be elected. And, if I.B.M. or General Electric is concerned about the behavior of the wives of their executives, perhaps they should be encouraged to pay the corporation wife a salary for keeping their executives in good spirits and good repair. These wives might perform better for incentive pay.

It would be worthwhile to examine further the role of the American corporation wife, since the women who become wives of managerial-level businessmen and the women who become professionals generally are drawn from the same pool of educated middle- and upper-class women. The corporation wife's role is a prototype of the ancillary role the woman often plays in her husband's career, no matter what the occupation, a position with elaborate role demands. The following is largely drawn from William Whyte's perceptive analysis of the corporation wife, as true today for many corporations as it was in the

[47] Helfrich, "The Generalized Role of the Executive's Wife," *Marriage and Family Living* 23–24 (1961), 384–387.

1950's. Whyte makes clear the pressures on the women, as well as the wives' own cooperation in their submission to controls.[48] He sees the process as one of socialization with self-selection. He maintains that "Management . . . deliberately plans and creates a favorable, constructive, attitude on the part of the wife that will liberate her husband's total energies for the job." These characteristics apparently are strongly internalized by the younger women. Among older executives there is a strong feeling that the wives of their aspiring junior executives (aged 25 to 40) are on the whole more cooperative than the older wives.

Whyte writes that women's own conception of the proper wifely role has given rise to the image of the ideal corporation wife. From comments gathered from wives of executives, he points out that the role stresses the negative — what the good wife should *not* do. She does not complain when her husband works late, does not fuss when a transfer comes up, does not engage in controversial activities, and "resolutely" is not a feminist. "The executive wife conceives her role to be that of 'stabilizer' — the keeper of the retreat, the one who rests and rejuvenates the man for the next day's battle." [49] She is expected to integrate with the local community, to become a civic leader, to provide a way-station on the route of the company boss on tour.

There is no question as to her primary obligation or her right to autonomy: "A serious career can be dismissed easily." Nor is the wife encouraged to help her husband in any but "wifely" duties. Wives who have donated money of their own to raise the family's living standard may provoke sanctions against the husband,[50] so that the middle-class working wife does not even have the working-class woman's legitimate option of working for added income.

[48] William H. Whyte, "The Wife Problem," *Life* (January 7, 1952), reprinted in Winch, McGinnis, and Baringer (eds.), *Selected Studies in Marriage and Family* (New York: Harcourt, Brace and Co., 1953), p. 118.
[49] *Ibid.*, p. 113. See also Helfrich, *op. cit.*
[50] Whyte, *op. cit.*, pp. 118, 120.

In the view of many companies, the wife should be integrated into the company. The most successful and conspicuous example has been set by I.B.M., which, following the policy set by Thomas Watson, has expected wives to be "all part of the business." "The good wife subordinates her own character and her aspirations to the smooth functioning of the system; she 'adapts.'" It is fortunate that the men who join the corporation come equipped with an amenable philosophy.[51]

The doctor's wife and lawyer's wife share many of the obligations of the corporation wife. Rossi's data show the relationship between the work of the wives and the demands of the husbands' occupational status on them.[52] Only small proportions of the wives of top professionals — doctors, lawyers, engineers, and scientists — work at all, much less have "careers" (16 percent of the doctors' wives, 25 percent of the scientists'). In contrast, 44 percent to 47 percent of the wives of librarians, social workers, and school teachers are employed.[53] If he falls into this second job grouping, the husband's occupational role probably entails fewer obligations on the wife's part; librarians and teachers have no need to attract and hold clients, nor do social workers care to have their clients associate at all with their families.

More than self-selection and indoctrination is at work here; the key factor may be the strongly held views of the future executives as to the kind of women they will marry. College-trained men, who constitute the pool from which executive trainees are selected, indicated in a National Opinion Research Center study that women should not choose a career difficult to combine with child-rearing.[54] They disapproved of women working when they had preschool children and were two to

---

[51] *Ibid.*, pp. 121, 124–125.

[52] Rossi, "Women in Science: Why So Few?" *Science* (May 28, 1965), p. 1198. Of course those husbands in occupations which require the participation of the wife also have higher incomes, and therefore women at these levels feel less economic pressure to work.

[53] *Ibid.*, p. 1199.

[54] Rossi, "Barriers to the Career Choice of Engineering, Medicine or Science Among American Women," *op. cit.*, p. 88.

three times more likely than a similar sample of women to say there was no need at all for the major recommendations made by the President's Commission on the Status of Women: increased child-care facilities, equal opportunities in hiring and promotion, and encouragement of more women to enter the professions and national political life.

Limitations of the Institutional Structure

The American woman faces her major impediment to a career in obligations she has and feels as a result of her statuses as wife and mother. Another important barrier lies in the power, authority, and ranking structure of the American social system, today more simplistically known as the Establishment. Women may be involved in the Establishment and essential to its smooth functioning, but only rarely do they occupy positions of power and authority within it. The problems they face in reaching such positions arise because vested interests fight to maintain the status quo and social pressures act to maintain the system as it has been.

Although some institutions change easily with the times, others seem more resistant to change. Women who respond to progress in the occupational world may find that the institution of the family is slower to change. Reconciling the disharmonies becomes a problem which the individual must face alone.

One can gain some insight by application of the "power" terminology so popular today.

Vested Interests in the Role Network

Goode is one social analyst who has indicated that men are loath to grant women opportunities to challenge their power positions.[55] Their opposition is not ideologically based but "interest" based. Because men typically have more power, they suspect and fear encroachment on that power. The situation is, of course, analogous to the fears of whites about retaining job

[55] Goode, *The Family*, p. 74.

priorities in the face of advancing opportunities for Negroes.[56] Hacker has claimed that discrimination against women arises from the "present contravention of the sexes," and outlines a number of types of opposition men display in the face of their "doubts and uncertainties concerning women's character, abilities and motives."[57] Many working women have firsthand knowledge of the responses of the threatened male, husband or employer, responses such as restraining, hindering, and upsetting their plans in managing work and home, often with the excuse that it is in the best interests of the woman. In fact, both the men and women in role network of the career-seeking woman may have interests in keeping her out of the occupational sphere and will put pressure on her to remain occupied with her home.

Let us examine the sources of negative pressures which arise from women's role networks and those which are culturally built in.

Husbands who may stand to lose on a number of levels if their wives work. The husband may need his wife to be available to promote his own success. As we have seen, she must be ready for business entertaining or to free him from time-consuming tasks (shopping for clothes, planning trips, maintaining links with his kin, and administering the home).

The husband may also feel threatened by the possibility that a working wife could outrank him in occupation or level of success. In American society the man whose wife is more prominent than he is, is usually pitied.[58] His position may be threatened even within the home. Most men are in an economically dominant position as breadwinner in the household and are usually the final decision-makers.

[56] For a further comparison see Helen Mayer Hacker, "Women as a Minority Group," *Social Forces* 30 (1951–52), 60–69.

[57] *Ibid.*, p. 67.

[58] The problems of rank disequilibrium and some mechanisms women lawyers use for coping with it in situations where they outrank their husbands are dealt with in my dissertation, "Women and Professional Careers," chapter 7.

There seems to be a curvilinear relationship between male dominance in the household and class position. It is lowest among the lower classes and increases with class level until it drops as it approaches the upper class, where the woman may command independent economic resources by inheritance. Thus, particularly in the middle class, the wife may in fact make most household decisions but most concede the right of the husband to a final veto. An index to the normative mandate requiring the wife's deference to the husband in important matters are the many jokes and folk wisdoms which instruct the wife how to "get around" her husband. The husband may demand his "rights"; the wife must wheedle. But a number of studies have indicated that where the wife also has command over economic resources, that is, if she works, her decision-making power in the household increases.[59] Her income, especially if it is greater than his, can undermine the basis for his authority over both her and the family as a whole.

The husband of a working wife may feel genuinely deprived compared to other husbands he knows and may well be absolutely deprived (he may, for example, have more household tasks to do). Practically, the husband requires a wife-surrogate when his wife is not present or is only a part-time wife, just as the child needs a surrogate for an absent mother. But the wife will usually be unwilling to find herself substituted for. The surrogate-wife is hardly an institutionalized role in the United States (those substitutes the husband picks usually are given other names). Thus the husband may make do with less by choice or by becoming resigned to it even though it is hardly in his interest to do so. And, although they might not be willing to admit it, some husbands may feel threatened by sexual competition from the men their wives encounter in the course of their work. Keeping women home-bound; segregating them in

---

[59] For example, Robert O. Blood, "The Husband-Wife Relationship," in F. Ivan Nye and Lois Wladis Hoffman, *The Employed Mother in America* (Chicago: Rand McNally & Co., 1963), p. 294.

suburbia where their only companionship is obtained from women in the same straits is as good a social structural device as India's purdah for keeping them locked into marriage. Though the housewife may meet many men in the course of a day, they are not typically from her own class. The husband faces real competition only when his wife is in contact with men from her own class who share her interests and tasks. The middle-class woman might run away with a corporate vice president, but she is not likely to run away with the laundry man. (A wife may also feel threatened by her husband's contacts with women in the work world. His daily association with a secretary who is either from a different social class and/or age category may not threaten too much because the relationship is normatively defined as necessary to the work. But like it or not, wives are in no position to do much about their feelings of insecurity.)

On the other hand, there may be, of course, considerable payoff in terms of shared interests, the "halo effect" to the husband of his wife's success, and the luxuries that added income may buy. The husband may also feel no loss if his wife performs all her roles with deep commitment and high energy but, as yet, such perfectly balanced relationships are rare.

Housewives who see the working woman as a threat to themselves.[60] The threat is varied. Career women are seen as competitors for their husbands (the working woman, though deprecated, also seems more glamorous — and often is, because she usually takes care of her appearance and is more interesting). The career also provides an alternate model to the domestic life and may cause the housewife to question her own choice of life style.

Parents, who may feel uncomfortable at having a career-minded daughter. Although parents usually derive satisfaction

---

[60] Arnold Rose, in "The Adequacy of Women's Expectations for Adult Roles," makes an analogy between these women and those who opposed women's suffrage.

from the mobility of a son, they may feel more ambivalent about their daughter's occupational success. The career-woman/daughter sometimes must be explained away or apologized for, lest friends believe they have produced an unfeminine daughter. Success is measured by the daughter's performance of the more traditional female roles. But parents may demonstrate considerable after-the-fact recognition because they do not assume their daughter will be successful. Once she has "arrived" they feel a deep sense of pride and forget having put emotional obstacles in her way or having chosen to assist their son in preference to their daughter.

Children, who more than any other group cannot perceive any personal advantage in the career of their mother. This attitude tends to vary, however, with the social environment of the child. We would expect youngsters who are reared with other children of working mothers to experience a lesser sense of relative disadvantage. However, those who grow up in communities where only a small percentage of mothers work might be expected to exert strong pressures on their mothers not to work.

Problems Caused by Stratification

Mechanisms which support stratification deter women's participation in high-ranking careers. Women derive rank first from their fathers and later from their husbands. This process works to keep families unified and is useful and necessary for the socialization of the children. Another consequence, however, is that it makes for a closed caste system for the married woman. Given our system, in which work is one of the prime determinants of rank position, it would indeed be "bad" if the woman achieved a high-ranking job, one higher than her husband's. Confusion would arise over her proper social niche. This is true to some extent also for the woman who outranks her husband socially by birth. A husband can raise a lower-ranking wife to his level without much disturbing the stratification system, provided, of course, that she can assume social graces appropriate for the rank.[61]

But when the husband is of lower social rank than the wife, he will rise only with difficulty and will experience and cause distress in social relations. There are few norms which guide the higher-ranking network in dealing with the lower-ranking aspirant: women may be absorbed; it is far more difficult to accept a man.

Institutions — The Pressures and Their Needs

A striking social obstacle to the utilization of woman-power in the occupational sphere comes from their participation in other institutions. The most obvious demands are, of course, those made by the family, described above. But changes in the economic structure of American society also have engaged women's time in other restrictive ways by enlarging the scope of the female role.

That women are probably the main agents of consumption in American society is an observation that social philosophers (including those on the left) fail to decry but that the advertising experts of Madison Avenue know well. Betty Friedan examined the implications of feminine spending in a chapter of *The Feminine Mystique* that never evoked popular excitement. She asked:

Why is it never said that the . . . really important role that women serve as housewives is *to buy more things for the house?* In all the talk of femininity and women's role, one forgets that the real business of America is business. But the perpetuation of housewifery, the growth of the feminine mystique, makes sense (and dollars) when one realizes that women are the chief customers of American business.[62]

[61] Elinor Barber describes the phenomenon for another historical period in *The Bourgeoisie in 18th Century France* (Princeton, N.J.: Princeton University Press, 1955).

[62] Betty Friedan, *The Feminine Mystique*, pp. 206–207.

Of course there is a "chicken-or-the-egg" question involved here: Do American women, because of greater leisure time, devote themselves to perusing the marketplace, or are there important pressures which direct them to devote more time to it because the economy, built on consumption, obsolescence, and replacement, depends on this essentially feminine activity? There is no doubt that, whether or not this activity is an intended or an unanticipated consequence of our economic system, prosperity and production would probably falter if women were to spend more time with ideas rather than with furniture, clothing, and the popular media.

It is also part of the wife's role to adorn herself and her home as an attestation of the husband's rank. We can expect that activity in this area increases with socio-economic level.

It is not necessary to our analysis to consider the dynamics of the economic system, or even to question whether or not alternative modes of consumption could guarantee the United States an equally high standard of living; we need only point out its implications for the woman's time budget and life style.

Consider some implications of the fact that in American society woman's primary economic role has come to be that of a consumer.

In the sex division of labor, women have been allocated the purchasing role in the United States, important because a large part of the culture is built around consumption. Shopping is a popular activity, legitimized by the value attached to intelligent shopping — getting good value and bargains. The value of clever shopping seems to be rated higher than the value of the time spent on it, which, in the case of housewives, is rarely calculated in the total cost. Of course, the shopping syndrome is made possible by the large amount and variety of goods available in the society and the money and credit available for purchases.

In contrast, Soviet and Chinese society are not consumer societies. Perhaps they will become so in time, but they do not now have an array of goods to consume. Therefore the consumer's role does not have to be filled by persons of any particular social category. In a sense, women in the Soviet Union gain from their society's deprivation. Even the Russian counterpart of the corporation wife cannot ordinarily buy a large house and devote herself to decorating it. Though people wish to have consumer goods, their acquisition is still sharply limited by availability, time, money, and space in which to put them. Families live in cramped quarters, and apartments often shelter several generations of a family or even several families.[63] Women living in these conditions can hardly reinforce each other's addiction to home improvements. For the Soviet woman truly to express herself, she must follow the male pattern — through work.

To the extent to which business acknowledges and encourages women's institutionalized role as consumers, it has a vested interest in keeping the costs of women's professional activity high. Professional women are less consumer-oriented; they have less time to buy and be pre-occupied with purchasing, and they have not generally been a target group for advertising. We do not know whether working women in fact spend less than housewives of the same class. Women lawyers interviewed for my study did not report spending a significant percentage of their time on shopping; they did make substantial purchases and used personal services such as professional laundries and caterers, and, of course, they often bought expensive clothing. As yet, however, business has not produced specifically for the market oriented to the career woman and therefore appears to be not interested in selling to it.

The Economics of Working

American society finds its rationale for work in the Protestant ethic: work is a means of livelihood rather than an avenue for self-expression or self-realization. So the case against the

---

[63] See David Granick, *Red Executive* (New York: Doubleday, 1963), for a description of how middle-managerial people in the Soviet Union live.

middle-class married woman who works is often put in economic terms: "Does it *pay* her to work?" Only rarely will it go beyond, to "does it benefit society?" "Does she want to work?" or some similar question. The reply is expected to be measured in terms of the high expenses incurred by the woman for child-care services, added clothing, daily work expenses, domestic help, expenditure for high-cost convenience foods, and the difference between the cost of her convenience shopping and the full-time housewife's comparison shopping.

The incomes of working women are taxed at the same rate as men's and often at higher rates if they are added to the husbands', as they are on most family tax returns. Although the cost of child care is the most fundamental of a working mother's business expenses, tax relief for child care is available only to those women in the very lowest economic strata. Child care alone can consume a considerable portion of the working mother's salary. (Although much has been said publicly on this issue, including a recommendation of the President's Commission on the Status of Women to liberalize existing provisions for tax exemptions,[64] no implementing legislative action has been taken. This suggests a rather low priority given to it by society.)

Thus, work pays only those women who must work (and perhaps depend on free baby-sitting from kin) and the relatively rare highly paid woman professional. When the family's books are balanced, the typical woman's work is not likely to show a sizeable economic return, at least when compared to that of her husband. Further, the weighing of potential economic return is usually applied to the woman early in her life, when the possibility of substantial financial gain seems — and is — remote. It seems a reasonable assumption that many lower-income families will strain their budgets to help a son through college while declining to pay any part of a girl's expenses; it is further likely that many girls from poorer families,

---

[64] *Report of the Commission on the Status of Women* (Washington, D.C.: U.S. Government Printing Office, 1963).

realizing the difficulty of earning all their own expenses, never seriously consider college.[65]

In addition, girls do not ask for financial help even when it is available. In James Davis's *Great Aspirations* study of bright students going on to graduate schools, only 18 percent of the men but 41 percent of the women did not apply for stipends. Of those who did not apply, 47 percent of the brightest men were not going on to graduate school for financial reasons; 38 percent of the brightest women did not go on.[66]

In a discussion of the work of President's Committee on Education Beyond High School, Anna Hawkes has commented: "Very few girls will mortgage their future for the present education. They will not saddle their husbands-to-be with the cost of their education, and they are fearful they will not be able to repay the debt before they marry. For boys, borrowing for their education is a definite investment in their future." [67] Girls who go to college generally depend on their parents for financial support; Havemann and West report that of the girls in their sample only one in six earned one-half or more of their own expenses as opposed to five-sixths of the boys who partially or entirely paid for their own education.[68]

The evidence suggests that while the daughter of the upper-stratum family has the same access to higher education that her brother has (although not to professional training), the goals of the daughter of the lower-strata family will be sacrificed as a matter of course to give her brother the opportunity at college training.

It is likely that where the family is under financial strain it will find ways to pay for a boy's medical or other professional education, and then will elicit assistance from other kin to buy

[65] Havemann and West, *op. cit.*, p. 15; and Goode, *World Revolution and Family Patterns*, p. 14.
[66] James A. Davis, *Great Aspirations.* Volume I: "Career Decisions and Educational Plans During College," p. 499.
[67] Anna L. Rose Hawkes, "Factors Affecting College Attendance," in Opal D. David (ed.) *The Education of Women*, p. 31.
[68] Havemann and West, *op. cit.*, p. 18.

equipment to put him in practice. This is probably not true for the girl, even if her feelings of commitment are strong, except in a markedly better family economic situation. (One governing factor may be the girl's marriage prospects at the time she enters her profession. If her prospects are poor, she may have a better chance for aid, but if she is about to be married her family may refuse to help her.) Parents who expect to reap benefits in their old age from investment in a son may not feel they can count on such support from a daughter's success.

This type of economic reasoning is a strong element in the sequence of decisions that leads most girls to liberal arts programs in college. Training in a technical specialization is not considered a good investment for a girl. Technical training is specific training, and the more specific the training, the more real the sense of impending waste—if a woman marries and does not work, the specialized training is unusable. (Women lawyers who leave law often claim their training in logical thinking is useful in everyday life, but none is able to use her specific knowledge of the law in more than peripheral ways.)

Many assume that the woman will not practice in the field in which she has been trained, or if she does that her career will lack continuity. It is true that this career pattern is followed by many professionally qualified women. But the pattern, though the understandable result of many pressures, cannot reasonably be held to be inevitable or to be a justification, on economic grounds, for a veto of effective career planning. The failure to plan effectively is often a result of cultural attitudes toward the value of time and money and priorities for spending which are economically nonrational.

It is true that usually little or no thought is given to the investment necessary early in many women's careers for child and household care, even though this is an investment likely to be returned with interest as the woman advances in her work. Thus, while a male doctor expects to go into debt to buy equipment for an office or to pay for his training, a woman doctor may not feel as free to borrow in addition to pay a housekeeper, an essential part of what she requires to build a practice. It is also probably true that if her family did not have resources, a bank would not give a loan for this specific purpose, though perhaps this has not been tested. Even when women are given fellowship aid for studies, they are reluctant to use it for child care or other household help. Very likely she will drop or delay her work because she cannot afford to be free to work. (Hanna Papenek suggests [69] that because there is not enough work in the modern American home to keep a housekeeper busy full time, it is not considered worthwhile to pay her to be around in case she is needed, *even if one can afford it*.)

The problem varies, however, with the type of work. Doctors can count on a good income in the early years of practice; attorneys, however, usually do not reach a comparable level until their practices are well established, perhaps not until late middle age. Thus the woman doctor may have far better economic reasons to stick to her practice than the woman lawyer who knows that economic reward still is far away. This may also be the reason why women lawyers, far more than men, seek salaried positions.

It is precisely in the years in which a woman most needs household help that she is also most apt to make the least money. Unless she plans well ahead and has vision and confidence, she may be unable to succeed. (Many professional women I interviewed did not face this problem because they married late and had children after their careers were well established.)

But there is no doubt that the professional woman who does make the early investment can make work pay. We would expect, therefore, that those women who have families and also build successful professional lives do not fall prey to the dominant attitudes concerning the economics of women's work. Almost any professional makes more money than a domestic em-

---

[69] As quoted by Lotte Bailyn, *op. cit.*, p. 706.

ployee, and each additional year of practice means an increased income.

Vested Interests of the Middle-Class Woman

The secondary gains of American middle-class housewives are of no small consequence to the fact that they shun careers and professional lives. In a sense their situation can be compared with that of other groups which have been denied full access to the opportunities of the society.

Though it is not commonly stressed, some disadvantaged groups have been protected from the full consequences of their position. This was true for those Negro slaves whose owners cared for them in times of ill health and old age. Similarly, secondary gains are experienced by crippled and sick persons who find that their disabilities may be useful if they wish to use them as instruments to control and regulate the lives of those close to them. The disabled are also free from the stresses most face in this achievement-oriented society and may, with an unchallengable excuse, retreat from competing.

For many disadvantaged persons, these advantages are small or no compensation; the directions in which they are led may be ill-suited to their temperament or ambitions. Historically, the protectiveness of the slave-owner was no deterrent to the slave's quest for freedom. However, short-term gains may cause less of a focus on long-term goals. They may even result in behavior unattached to goals.

The American middle-class woman has a substantial interest in the status quo. This commitment is clearly linked to the secondary gains that have accrued to her, seemingly as rewards for service to her class, her husband, and her society. Consider the wide range of these gains.

RANK

To the extent that her husband is successful, the American woman need not concern herself with building or maintaining rank in society. She simply takes as her own the rank achieved through her husband's success. (Of course, it is no gain to her if her husband does not achieve respectable rank, but nevertheless she rides tandem with him on the road to success *or* failure.)

PUBLIC ATTENTION

To the extent that her husband is successful, the wife will gain attention irrespective of her own qualities (although these can, of course, enhance the demand for her presence). Mrs. Richard Nixon, for example, recently was the recipient of an honorary Doctor of Laws degree from Finch College, although she had not participated notably in any occupational or artistic activities. As wife of the then Republican candidate for president, she had achieved "fame." Hers is but one of the numerous cases of women who rise to public attention when their husbands attain success; they become subjects for feature articles in women's magazines and national magazines such as *Life* or *Time*.

LEISURE TIME

If the woman chooses to use domestic help to care for her home and children, she has considerable freedom to pursue individual interests in the arts, athletics, and social activities. However, her freedom is somewhat limited, and should a hobby develop into a vocational interest she may encounter considerable opposition. She may, however, schedule her time as she pleases and is limited only by the schedules of her children and husband.

LACK OF ECONOMIC PRESSURE TO WORK

The woman is freed from pursuing a vocation and, short of a family economic crisis, she is not expected to contribute to the joint finances. Should she want to work, she need not make a great deal of money. Thus, because she doesn't have to, the woman has a choice of either voluntary work or work for pay.

LOWERED STANDARDS

The middle-class woman is required to operate at only minimum capacity. So far as achivement is concerned, it is likely
that anything she does outside of the home — from P.T.A. and
charity work to a part-time job or participation in politics —
will be regarded as extra and evidence that she is a superior
person. (Although standards for housekeeping performance
have undoubtedly gone up, it is doubtful that a plain cook will
suffer criticism; rather, a gourmet cook will be praised.)

If the middle-class woman enters the occupational world, she
is not judged by the same standards as her husband. Working
women receive more praise and notice at a lower rank in the
occupational hierarchy than a man would, and for a lower level
of performance as well.[70] This gain has a clear drawback. She
gets more for doing less, but is more satisfied with less and has
less incentive to aim higher. George Homans describes this
phenomenon as "occupational justice," since "by the standards
current in American industry, the female sex is considered to
have made a lower investment than the male, and so by dis-
tributive justice, to deserve a less good job than the male." [71]

THE PATTERN OF REVOCABILITY

As we pointed out in Chapter I, American women have
cultural approval to "cop out." Those women who choose to
leave an occupation or profession at any level, from training
to practice, may do so with society's full approval and will be
given credit for having reached whatever level they have attained, though a man in a similar situation would be considered a failure. We found that women ex-lawyers were eagerly
sought after in their communities as P.T.A. presidents and club

[70] *Time* (March 6, 1964), p. 48, reporting on women in law, notes that
"Many Portias admit with a touch of asperity that they are often overpraised
by men for a performance that would be regarded as merely competent in
another male."

[71] *Social Behavior: Its Elementary Forms* (New York: Harcourt, Brace, and
World, 1961), pp. 236–237.

leaders. Male ex-lawyers who retire to a job with lower status would probably be ignored by community organizations.

The middle-class woman may have the freedom to devote a major portion of her time to personal adornment and attention to herself. Though some may criticize such narcissistic behavior, it is expected that a wife of a successful man should look her best, much in the same way that a man's efforts to improve his position are not seen as ego adornment but as an effort on behalf of his family. The woman need not work hard at adornment either; she needs only the taste and money to pick her beauticians and couturiers. In another culture this style of life might be considered parasitic, but to the extent that the woman enjoys it and can afford it, it is condoned in American society.

Middle-class and upper-class women can depend on income that bears no direct connection to their efforts, ability, or output. They have achieved, in effect, a guaranteed annual wage. They receive it because of their ascriptive status — wife. This definition is upheld by the social system; for example, in divorce actions, alimony for the wife is often calculated on the basis of the style of life her husband has provided her with before the separation.

Special Ecological Impediments

The way Americans choose to live, their suburban residential pattern, their geographical mobility, all have many consequences for women's work habits.

Women do not display the same mobility patterns as men. Although single women may travel to find work opportunities, once married they usually must follow their husbands. Women in large economic centers have more opportunity to train and work; the closer a woman lives to the center of the city, the more likely it is that she will work; conversely, the further she lives from the city, the less likely it is she will train or work.

Marilyn E. Stone, D.D.S., of the Association of American Women Dentists, reports that women in dentistry certainly locate their practices in urban centers.[72] Women lawyers in my study who practiced full-time tended to live in the central city; those who lived in the suburbs practiced part-time or not at all. This does not include those whose homes were in suburban towns having genuine business and commercial centers. This was found to be true also for women physicians, accountants, and even geographers.

Geographic location has direct consequences for the life patterns of educated middle-class women, most of whom live in suburbia. The most common contrast with the American pattern is the Swedish. The Swedes do not share our feelings that we deprive our children if we bring them up in the city; a vacation shack in the country generally satisfies the Swedish apartment-dweller's bucolic longings.[73] Alice Rossi claims that Swedish women find work and home easier to combine than American women do because Sweden has avoided the pattern of sprawling suburban developments in its postwar housing expansion. The emphasis in Swedish building has been on inner-city housing improvement. With home close to diversified services for schooling, child care, household help, and places of work, it has been much easier in Sweden than in the United States to draw married women into the labor force and keep them there.[74]

Contrast this with the pattern of recent American development.

The rapid suburbanization of residential America has not been accompanied by a parallel decentralization of educational or career opportunities. Professional centers remain urban, as

---

[72] Personal communication.
[73] Tomasson, *op. cit.*, p. 179.
[74] Rossi, "Equality Between the Sexes: An Immodest Proposal," *Daedalus* (Spring 1964), pp. 637–638.

do the great centers of learning, and suburban branches of both tend to be of lower caliber where they exist at all.

Suburban shopping centers have made it unnecessary for women to come to the central city where there are libraries, art museums, lectures, and, most important, stimulating events and people. Suburban women live in a kind of solitary confinement with those of their own kind.

Child-care services of all kinds are more available in the city. Domestic workers usually prefer to work in the city; probably more emergency child care is available through agencies and neighbors who are sympathetic to the needs of the working mother. In addition, many more private and public nurseries and schools operate in the city.

Though smaller communities offer less anonymity and one can know and depend on one's neighbors more, personal involvements and the requirements of reciprocity can consume more time and energy than they would in a city.

Women and Careers

Much of the strain experienced by the woman who attempts to work is structured strain, caused by a combination of an overdemanding set of role obligations, lack of consensus as to the hierarchy of obligations, and the clash of obligations from home and occupational statuses.

However, there are women who manage to fulfill a difficult combination of statuses. At the very least, they perform the basic role demands of each, though levels of efficiency and competence vary. The sets of mechanisms used to meet these demands may be categorized as follows:[75]

The elimination of social relationships.

The professional woman may deal with overdemanding and conflicting role obligations by eliminating social contact with

---

[75] Many of the responses follow the pattern that Merton has identified as the strain toward consistency. That is, where sectors of a social system are in conflict, there appear to be mechanisms at play which push for alleviation of the conflict.

specific persons,[76] not roles, but who generate difficulties in the role relationship. Although one may choose to marry and acquire the husband-wife role relationship, who the husband is and how he chooses to play the husband's role may make a considerable difference in whether or not the wife is placed under strain. The professional woman would do well to avoid the persons around her whose expectations cause most inconvenience to and most pressure on her. Included are those who would activate inappropriate statuses in the course of a task. For example, the friend who helps out by caring for the children one afternoon but who makes nasty comments about women who work, or the colleague in a law firm who thinks women ought to stay home and have no head for legal work.

Choosing friends and colleagues is important. The woman does best to surround herself with a circle who share professional and family statuses — other working mothers. If possible, she ought to have an overlapping person set of friends who are also co-workers. With respect to biased employers, she faces fewer obstacles if she avoids any firm known to object to woman employees; if she were to be employed by them, she would be faced with many assumptions about her performance based on her status as a woman rather than as a serious worker.

Reduction of the total number or amount of contacts involved in the role relationship (not elimination of the status or the role relationship altogether).

For example, a woman is a mother whether she has one, two, or three children, or more. Yet the number of children she has makes a substantial difference in terms of the total demands on her.[77] She may reduce the potential overload of strain by choosing to have a small family. Contrary to folktales that two

[76] David Caplovitz describes this as the "person-set" (that complement of persons who may hold the same status) in "Student-Faculty Relations in Medical School: A Study in Professional Socialization," unpublished Ph.D. dissertation (Columbia University, 1961), Appendix A.

[77] Yudkin and Holme, *op. cit.*, p. 54, show that mothers with one child are more apt to work than mothers who have two or more.

children are no harder to handle than one, each additional person makes additional demands. Three children means three birthday parties, three school plays, and three sets of clothing to launder; the percentage of output necessary may decrease with each child, but there is an absolute increase in time demands. The same may be true for the number of friends and many other relationships.

The number of statuses in the woman professional's status set.

Although expansion of the role set is a mechanism by which some reduce strain, the possession of a large number of statuses which entail real time allocations (as opposed to nominal statuses) can be a serious problem. If a woman can maintain a fairly small number of statuses, she will be less deflected in the performance of her professional and home roles. This means that with the increase of obligations in one status (such as birth of a second child), a woman may have to reduce those of another (perhaps eliminating participation in voluntary or even professional organizations). To some extent she is playing a zero-sum game, that is, in order to perform adequately in one role, she must perform less than adequately in another.

The mechanism of redefinition.

The woman may redefine her occupational status as being an adjunct to her family statuses. In this way she not only overcomes psychological feelings of guilt, but also may legitimate her occupational role, both to herself and her family. Many women with active professional careers form partnerships with their husbands. There are many obvious advantages to this, not the least of which is that the woman who is in partnership with her husband may define her work goal as "helping her husband," rather than advancing her own career. Since it is culturally valued for the wife to be a helpmate, her occupational activity will not be considered self-indulgent. Similarly, if she defines her motives for working as economically essential for the family, she receives legitimation for "doing it for the family."

Such redefinition of role behavior may not only reduce strain considerably, but it also has the negative consequence of undermining the woman's occupational commitment, circumscribing her activities and limiting her in areas and subspecialties which do not lend themselves to redefinition. A woman who is a law partner with her husband may say she is only helping him, but she can hardly aim at a judgship on the same ground.

Intermittent activation of statuses.[78]

The woman who can do one job at a time, that is, be a mother at home and a doctor in the office without allowing any overlap, eliminates a lot of problems. Although not all women can rely on this mechanism, depending on the contextual setting it can be used flexibly as needed. For example, if the woman has children of summer-camp age, a decision to send them to camp means she can be temporarily relieved of the mother status. For some persons, among them writers, painters, and academic women who do not have time for research in the winter, this time may be crucial.

Similarly, if she chooses an occupation with slow periods and vacations, she may have more opportunity to activate her mother status. As a teacher she has summers free to be with children; as a psychiatrist she has a month or two of vacation; if she is self-employed as a lawyer or free-lance writer, she may manipulate her schedule throughout the year to activate the status most needed at any given time.

Compartmentalization by scheduling.

The woman might adopt a rigid nine-to-five work schedule permitting no evening or weekend activities, or she might arrange work so that it was close to home to permit better and more coordinated work-home activities. It may well be that a woman's facility in being able to suspend one status while en-

---

[78] This is akin to Goode's mechanism of compartmentalization. "A Theory of Role Strain," *op. cit.*, p. 486.

gaged in activation of another would be of even more importance in dealing with role strain than it would be for the man. His statuses are apt to have more congruent demands and his occupational role usually has a clear priority. Thus, for the female doctor to be her husband's social hostess for an evening (to be a wife and exclude her occupational status) is of great importance if she wants to meet expectations attached to her wife-mother roles without intrusion from her professional life. The woman who is in the limelight at a party because she is pretty and charming has far less trouble with her husband than the one who holds an audience by her recitation of business coups.

Delegation of tasks and roles.

The woman who chooses excellent (although it may be expensive) help for her home tasks has a better chance of performing both occupational and family roles well than the woman who relies on part-time or nonprofessional help. In addition, the more help she has (though probably there is a point of diminishing return), the less strain will she be under. The most successful working women interviewed employed two in help so that, as they explained, each of the two could be relied upon to cover essential tasks if the other became ill. For the mechanism to work, delegation must be professional; selection must be routinized and quality evaluated in advance. Haphazard arrangements only add to strain, although any one crisis may come out all right. In a study conducted for the Bureau of Vocational Information in 1925, Collier found that 42 percent of the one hundred professional and business mothers she interviewed had two or more full-time domestic servants to maintain their homes and take care of their children during the day; only nine of these one hundred women had no full-time servants, and five of them had their mothers living with them.[79]

[79] Virginia MacMakin Collier, *Marriage and Careers: A Study of One Hundred Women Who Are Wives, Mothers, Homemakers and Professional Women* (New York: The Channel Bookshop, 1926), pp. 59, 74.

Although there are no comparable statistics on contemporary professional women (other than the fact that they are more apt to pay for help than women in lower income brackets), observations indicate, and statistics on the decline in the domestic labor force confirm, that contemporary business and professional women have less than professional domestic-help arrangements.[80] Younger middle-class women today, carrying the standard of equality, find it difficult to employ and use servants efficiently.

In addition, we would expect to find that professional women delegate much of the consumer role to others. We would expect them to exhibit less preoccupation with amassing "things."

The increasing observability of role demands.[81]

If the professional woman becomes well known in a community because of organizational activity, as in the P.T.A. or a local political club, she may be excused from being asked to do any number of friend-neighbor-community and even family tasks because people "know how busy she is." The main danger of this mechanism is overextension and consequent loss of control over time and social obligations.

Expansion of the role set is effective, however, only if the woman permits the system to help her. As was pointed out in Chapter I, many women in professional life complicate their time budgets by insisting on fulfilling all the obligations attached to their various roles (including much participation in school organizations and extensive family activities) to prove that they are successful wives and mothers as well as profes-

---

[80] Low and Spindler, *Child Care Arrangements of Working Mothers in the United States.* Henry C. Zazewski, *Child Care Arrangements of Full-Time Working Mothers* (Washington, D.C.: U.S. Department of Health, Education and Welfare, 1959), Children's Bureau Publication 378.

[81] Here we are using the mechanism of observability of the individual role activities, and observability of conflicting roles by members of the role set mechanisms outlined by Merton to facilitate the individual's performance of roles. "The Role Set: Problems in Sociological Theory," *British Journal of Sociology* 8 (June 1957), 113 *ff.*

sional women. Where such a woman does not limit the demands on her by permitting herself to be excused from many of them, she is apt to experience considerable strain.

Reliance on rules (or appeals to "third parties") for legitimation of role behavior.

As in bureaucracies, where managers may use rules to depersonalize a command or reproach, as in referring to a command as coming from "above," women too may use work rules when challenged at home. In a sense this is an aspect of delegation. The publisher's deadline for the woman writer may impress her husband so that he relaxes his social schedule to permit her more time to meet the demands of the outside rules. The obligation to meet office hours or class hours are similar outside rules family members respect and defer to.

Women and Careers: Social Structures That Help

In addition to the personal decisions individual women may make to resolve role conflict, there are built-in social structural arrangements which may reduce the possibility of role strain and make it easier for women to perform their professional roles. Always the context in which each occurs is important because, depending on specific circumstances, the same arrangements that help one woman may hinder another's attempt to work.

SHARED STATUSES

To the extent that women share statuses with others in their role set they may be expected to suffer less role strain than those who share fewer statuses. In the following examples, shared statuses reduce role-strain.

The women who shares statuses (other than sex) with colleagues and clients:

If a woman is a member of a Wall Street law firm, her presence probably will arouse less resistance if she, like her colleagues, is white, Protestant, from an upper-class background, a graduate of an Ivy League college and law school, and a resident of an upper-class community. This would apply as well to male members of the firm, but the appropriate complement of personal characteristics may be more crucial for the woman. The tradition-bound gatekeepers of the old law firms who object to women attorneys probably are more comfortable with a woman who is "one of them" in all ways except sex. The same is true for women professionals in small localities who share the ethnic status and school and neighborhood background of their clients; this makes the building of a professional practice easier and ongoing interpersonal relations less strained. Shared statuses also make for greater visibility of the woman's problems. Since the obligations of her other statuses are known to those people with whom she is in interaction, they may be more aware of her need for flexibility in professional role performance.

Shared practices. The woman who works with her husband:

If spouses are aware of the duties each must perform during the work day, the demands of work, home, and social life will be clear to both and they can cope with them in a fluid and workable way. There are, of course, couples who find it difficult to work together, although most women lawyers and doctors with whom I have spoken report enthusiastically on work relationships with husbands and a few couples in scientific research have corroborated this. In all of these cases, the husband is the acknowledged head of the team.

Shared Fields. The women whose husband is in the same or similar field:

Bailyn suggests that "the circumstance of a woman's working professionally in the same field as her husband . . . reduces the burdens of keeping up with the field, of maintaining contact within it, and decreases the need for an independent institutional affiliation." [82] The advantages may ac-

[82] Bailyn, *op. cit.*, p. 708.

crue to both partners: many doctors who marry nurses benefit
by their shared orientation to the medical field and their
knowledge of the workaday demands within it. But these
benefits may be offset. Many colleges and universities have
rules which prohibit husbands and wives from working in the
same department or the same school, and in such situations the
wife will usually defer to her husband's career.

The woman whose friends are in a similar field:

If friends are colleagues the woman's professional role will
be reinforced. Although it seems to be usual for professional
women to seek friends among their female colleagues, few may
be near at hand and it may be difficult for the professional
woman to locate a congenial companion. Soviet women may
find it easier to find female friends in their field, for Soviet students are assigned dormitory accommodations according to academic discipline [83] and are more likely to form permanent
professional friendships in school.

Defining Statuses as Complementary

Less role strain will exist where the statuses within the status
set are complementary by definition.

The woman may avoid role conflict entirely where there is
cultural approval of her statuses and they are defined as being
complementary. The case is clear where women choose to practice in the so-called feminine fields. Bailyn has outlined some of
the positive consequences of performing professional work "devoted to problems and concerns that the woman herself faces in
her private capacity within the family." Some of these fields are
education, pediatrics, certain forms of psychiatry, social work,
and, of course, nursing. She asserts: "By lessening the distance
between her two roles and hence reducing the contradictions in
her self-image it would be expected to ease her problems." But,

[83] Information from Kama Koslova (Soviet exchange student) at the Bryn
Mawr conference on the Role and Status of Women in Soviet Russia.

she adds: "It might also lead to a weakening of her intellectual forces by blurring the distinction between work and family life, and create special disturbances in her family role by introducing a degree of external authority incommensurate with the natural conduct of that role." [84] There is no doubt, however, that a girl will meet more encouragement for training in these fields, and even receive genuine assistance in working in them.

Role Relaxation

Where the obligations of one or more statuses are underdemanding, the possibility of role strain will be reduced.

Women sometimes find that the obligations attached to one or more of their statuses do not subject them to many pressures. Probably the woman who is a wife but has few wifely duties has the most freedom to pursue a career. (Just as those who have low-pressure jobs, not "careers," can probably pursue marriage with more dedication.) Since she is married she need not pursue a husband. But she may find that she can be a satisfactory wife without the investment of much time or energy, for example where the husband's work does not require his wife's assistance as hostess or helpmate, or in situations in which work takes so much of the husband's time that she is freed, without guilt, to pursue her own career. Of course, the absent husband makes the fewest demands. War, adventure, and some kinds of jobs may carry the man off for long periods, permitting the woman to be a wife yet relieving her of many wifely obligations. On the other hand, if the husband travels extensively, the wife may find that her burden increases because she may have to be responsible for a great many family obligations for which help is usually provided by the husband.

When children go out of town to college or camp, the woman similarly benefits from role relaxation. She may find that her active role as daughter may diminish if parents move

[84] Bailyn, *op. cit.*, pp. 708–709.

away or travel, or if siblings agree to share parental responsibilities.

Statuses in Name Only

The possibility of role strain will be reduced where a status is nominal rather than active.

This is the polar extreme of role relaxation; the best-known type is the wife-in-name-only, the woman who holds the status of wife but is not involved in it, and sometimes chooses to over-participate in her status as a professional. Some observers claim that women who turn to their work as a primary source of rewards do so because they have failed to find fulfillment as wives and mothers. They are accused of manifesting the psychological mechanism of compensation. Ruth Benedict, for example, according to Jessie Bernard, was escaping from an uncongenial marriage in her work.[85]

It is probably true that, faced with an unsatisfactory marriage, a woman, like a man, may seek compensation in work for the socio-emotional rewards she would normally have within the family. Some writers refer to the family as a tension-management unit of society,[86] but it clearly can also be a tension-provoking sector.

It is probably more difficult for a woman to maintain a bad marriage and the demands of work than it is a man. As long as the husband is present, the woman probably needs his good feelings and cooperation to combine her career and home obligations successfully; he can probably manage without her cooperation. Thus, we might expect to find that the marriages of professional women are either very successful or very bad. There are no statistics on successful marriages, but we know there is a higher divorce rate (role-strain resolution by elimination of a status) among professional women than among professional men. (See Table 8 above.)

---

[85] Bernard, *Academic Women*, p. 105.
[86] Talcott Parsons, in particular; see *The Social System* (Glencoe, Ill.: The Free Press, 1951).

Status Substitutes

The possibility of role strain will be reduced where the obligations of one or more statuses are assumed by surrogates who share enough attributes to be genuine substitutes.

The working woman who has a devoted mother or maiden aunt willing and competent to care for her child has a built-in reliable and inexpensive surrogate-mother. The grandmother-caretaker offers still other fringe benefits: she is devoted and loyal only to this family and loves the child. She is probably of equal social rank and is not likely to expose the child to improper manners, tastes, and attitudes (exception made for generational conflicts which occur in cases where grandmothers were immigrants to the United States). No opprobrium is attached to her caretaker role because she is not considered a domestic. Further, the mother will probably not feel jealous of her child's love for its grandmother since this is defined as a special relationship which should not be competitive. Of deep importance is the fact that the grandmother, co-opted [87] to the daughter's career plan, will probably provide emotional support and approval.

Highly Ranked Statuses

The higher the rank of the statuses in a woman's status set, the more easily she may be able to manage a greater number of statuses. This is probably true whether a total evaluation of rank (adding the rank of each status) of all statuses is used, or simply the rank of the occupational status (of the woman alone).

Rossi points out that "the higher the job level, the greater is the flexibility possible in the allocation of time . . . to be able to manipulate her hours freely is a very great asset to a woman

[87] Philip Selznick, *T.V.A. and the Grass Roots* (Berkeley: University of California Press, 1953), reported the co-opting mechanism as used by a government agency: local leaders were asked to participate in a program, and thus gave support in a situation where they might have been obstructionists.

holding a job, rearing children and homemaking." [88] Furthermore, the higher the social class from which a woman comes,
the more freedom she has (through access to money, facilities,
and servants) to pursue her own interests. (Riesman points out
that in many tradition-oriented societies, certain individuals are
encouraged toward individuality from childhood, especially if
they belong to families of high status.) [89] Similarly, if the
woman is of high social class, she is psychologically freer and
more accustomed to having and using the services of others. In
short, her social-class status may supersede her female status.
This has been offered as an explanation by Riesman for the
participation in political life of many upper-class women in societies which generally discriminate against women far more
than does the United States. In Pakistan, India, and Ceylon,
women have achieved much higher positions than in the Western world. The upper-class person may furthermore be permitted more bizarre behavior than the middle-class person; this
is of some consequence when the woman's professional activity
is classified as deviant and she must be psychologically free to
pursue her goals.

Riesman has also commented: "It seems possible that upper-
class position — and I mean here aristocratic values and not
simply more money — may give a few academic women a relative freedom from middle-class and lower-middle class conven-
tionalities concerning sex roles. It is clear . . . that academic
women, like college women in general, are of higher social ori-
gins than their male counterparts." [90] The late Queen Elisabeth
of Belgium (1876–1965) is a good example. The queen held an
M.D. degree from the University of Leipzig, earned before she
became the wife of the future King Albert. The role demands
of a queen are high and she did not, as a consequence, practice
medicine after her marriage, although she used her training to

[88] Alice S. Rossi, "A Good Woman Is Hard to Find," *Transaction* 2, No. 1
(November–December 1964), 20–23.
[89] Riesman, Glazer, and Denney, *The Lonely Crowd*, quoted in Alex Inkeles (ed.), *Readings on Modern Sociology*, p. 113.
[90] Introduction to Bernard, *Academic Women*, p. xx.

foster the improvement of health conditions in her country. (In addition to her high upper-class background she also had a substantial role model in the person of her father, Karl Theodor, Duke of Bavaria, who was an ophthalmologist.) [91]

Roles That Reinforce Each Other

In sum, where the network of role relations is supportive, role strain will be eliminated.

In the context of occupational choice and career development:

Hall has shown that family and friends play a significant role in envisaging the career line [92] and reinforcing the efforts of the recruit. He finds that they give encouragement, help establish appropriate routines, arrange for work privacy, discourage anomalous behavior, and define day-to-day rewards.[93]

Further, the supportive network feeds into the professional socialization process. Davis and Oleson have reported in their study of nurses that the significant others who accept and treat the woman as a professional help her to become secure in her occupational identity.[94]

Katz and Lazarsfeld's study found that "whether a person influenced another did not depend only upon the relation between the two, but also upon the manner in which they were imbedded into circles of friends, relatives or co-workers." [95] A Russian exchange student, M. Koslov, told the Bryn Mawr conference on Soviet women that friendship supports were impor-

---

[91] *Journal of the American Medical Association* 196 (April 18, 1966), 128.

[92] Oswald Hall, "The Stages of a Medical Career," *American Journal of Sociology* 53 (March 1948), 327–336.

[93] *Ibid.*, p. 328.

[94] "Whatever incipient, still very shaky identity they had acquired as nurses was buttressed by family and hometown friends who, much to the student's surprise, now approached them as specially knowledgeable and wise in matters related to health." Fred Davis and Virginia L. Oleson, "Initiation into a Woman's Profession: Identity Problems in the Status Transition of Coed to Student Nurse," *Sociometry* 26 (March 1963), 97.

[95] Elihu Katz and Paul F. Lazarsfeld, *Personal Influence: The Part Played by People in the Flow of Mass Communication* (Glencoe, Ill.: The Free Press, 1954), p. 7.

tant to Soviet women. She reported that when a woman dropped out of school, friends mobilized, pressuring her to return and offering assistance in the form of study-help.

Although a supportive structure is necessary for a man's success, women may depend on it even more, because of lack of firm initial motivation and inner direction. Even where early influences are strong, many pulls exist to divert women from careers at later stages of their lives.

In the context of the home and family:

An optimum career situation is most possible where family relations are in harmony, where the spouse favors the wife working and the children are in accord or at least indifferent to it. The woman is dependent on the emotional and practical support of all family members. They must often assume responsibilities that are culturally assigned to the woman and give up services that she can be legitimately asked to provide. Thus, it might be assumed that successful marriages, as measured by lack of friction between the spouses and an agreed division of labor, make a career for the woman a more viable possibility.

Roles Which Are Clear-Cut

The more role obligations are clearly defined, specified, and structured, the easier it will be to perform the role demands of a number of statuses. Certain occupations (and specialties within them) have structures that make the required tasks so specific that decisions as to whether one can or cannot perform them can be made even by the new recruit,[96] and the burden of constant and repeated time and resource allocation is eliminated. In medicine, for instance, office hours and appointments with patients are clearly defined obligations. So are the class hours of the academic woman, or the sequential time schedule of the female scientist involved in a biological experiment. This

---

[96] One cannot become a traveling salesman and then be surprised that work takes him from his family.

regularity also legitimates the time needed to prepare for work.[97] The pressures of meeting a court calendar, deadlines for submission of briefs, writs, and so on, define the time commitment necessary to fulfill the occupational role of lawyer.

In addition, curing the patient, or winning the case, gives the professional a clear knowledge that he has finished a task and is free to go on to another occupational activity or fulfill the obligations of another status. This is not so, for example, for the research sociologist, who usually never feels finished with a problem. The researcher further suffers from imprecise deadlines and unfocused sanctions, so that his tasks easily can be deferred to meet the demands of another role when they become pressing. The woman whose job holds strong and immediate sanctions (forfeiture by not appearing in court, losing the case, not getting paid) is able to organize her time more effectively than the woman whose job permits time encroachments from her other roles (the novelist or painter, for example).

This is equally true for decisions involved in the mother's role: if a child is ill and needs hospitalization there is no question but that the mother will leave her job and go to him (and no colleague will challenge her right and duty to do so), but if the child demands constant daily attention with minor complaints the mother may face a fresh and enervating decision each day.

The husband who tells his wife he does not object to her working if "she does what she thinks is right for him and the children" places more of an obstacle in her way than if he had made specific requests (such as two dinner parties a month for his clients and full responsibility for getting the children to school). The husband-wife relationship is such that a full detailing of tasks may not easily be made, but an attempt to regularize and standardize them would dispel ambivalence and the psychic toll resulting from role strain.

[97] This is partially a function of the obligations becoming "visible" to others and thus is one of the mechanisms Merton outlines in "articulating" the role set in "The Role Set," *op. cit.*

Status Obligations Which Bend to the Times

Where the burdens people face in fulfilling status obligations are highly visible, and society places a high priority on them, the institutional structures in which the tasks need to be done will bend to meet personal needs.

When shortages of manpower occur, for example, institutions which must employ women adjust their occupational demands to permit women to meet the demands of their home lives simultaneously. Examples are all-day nurseries attached to factories, more common in Europe than in the United States. In response both to their needs and to public notice of the problem, some American institutions have begun making provision for the children of their professional women staffs. In meeting the needs of women doctors, New York Medical College (The Metropolitan Hospital Center) has initiated a new program permitting part-time residence at the Department of Psychiatry.

There also has been discussion of changing nurses' hours to conform more to the hours of the school day. Nurses classically have worked a 7 A.M.–3 P.M. or 8–4 shift. If this could be altered to 9–5, child care would be simplified and more nurses would be able to work. Some of the obstacles to women's working come from traditional patterns of work hours and locations, habits usually not at all essential to the tasks involved. Many of these could be and are being changed to adapt to the needs of working mothers.

IV
THE STRUCTURE OF PROFESSIONS: HOW THEY AFFECT WOMEN'S PARTICIPATION

THE ways in which occupations are structured and the images and traditions associated with them have a profound effect on their selection by recruits and the ultimate success of the new people. The would-be recruit's racial, ethnic, and sex status have always been crucial to his ability to acquire and perform occupational roles in American society. This has been the experience of Negroes, Catholics, Jews, and women in professions which have been typically white, Protestant, and male. Those who have managed to jump color, ethnic, or sex barriers to enter a desired occupation find that success is difficult because they have not shared the same worlds as their colleagues and cannot count on them for the same assistance that people from the same backgrounds informally offer to one another. Further, the changes in traditions and images which today have begun breaking down racial and ethnic barriers do not yet seem to have had the same effect on the sex barrier.

In professions where men have predominated, being female has typically meant being unlike, and therefore unsuitable. Two processes ensure that this will happen: sex typing and status-set typing. In the professional context they are of major importance in setting and reflecting cultural expectations about the appropriateness of women's attainment of professional status and their subsequent performance as professionals. They are critical processes in the course of women's careers in the male-dominated professions.

Sex Typing of Occupations

According to Robert K. Merton, "occupations can be described as 'sex-typed' when a very large majority of those in them are of one sex and when there is an associated normative expectation that this is as it should be."[1] When occupations are sex-typed, the sex status of the person who is of the minority sex becomes as salient as, or more so than, the occupational status. The male lawyer in the courtroom evokes a set of responses geared to the legal task. The female lawyer, however, evokes a set of ambiguous responses in the same surroundings. Other lawyers and courtroom observers feel that her sex is somehow relevant to the performance of her job and that being female will alter the way she sees things and how she will act. They claim they cannot predict how she will act—unlike the male lawyer on whom they can rely to play by the "rules."

The sex typing of occupations (and the consequences for behavior it seems to entail) affects men where they are a distinct minority within an occupation, as in home economics or nursing. However, the consequences of sex typing in making sex status salient are magnified for women, and have generally inhibited their occupational success. Even where men constitute a minority in an occupation, they seem to have a better chance to do well and be upwardly mobile. Although the majority of

---

[1] Personal communication.

people in the professions of teaching and social work are women, men have proportionately more of the top administrative and supervisory posts. Where men constitute a very small minority, however, they may also suffer "discrimination." It was not until August of 1966 that the United States House of Representatives voted for equality of the sexes among nurses in the armed services, authorizing regular commissions for male nurses in the Army, Navy, and Air Force.[2]

The problems stemming from sexual imbalance are especially evident in the professions, and as we have seen in the Introduction,[3] in only a few of them has the disproportion of men and women shown any great change over the past fifty years. The rate of increase of women in the professions severely lags behind that for males. In nearly all instances, the number of women in the professions is not keeping up with the growth of their fields.

Sex typing of occupations occurs in all cultures. Some occupations become known as "male," others as "female," and some are not assigned to either sex. Each society rationalizes the appropriateness of these attributions[4] but societies vary greatly in whether a male or a female sex status is paired with a specific occupational status. Primitive societies sex-type such tasks as water carrying, gardening, hunting, and pottery making. Modern societies sex-type tasks such as typing, shoe making, letter carrying, and plumbing. All professions are sex-typed in American society. Nursing, social work, and elementary school teaching are female professions; law, medicine, the ministry, and architecture are male.

[2] *New York Times* (August 16, 1966).
[3] Table 1, p. 7, and Table 2, p. 8.
[4] Goode maintains that were the sex definition of occupations obvious there would be no rules about it. This is another case of his more general observation that "capacity is almost never the criterion for job allocation or efficiency" (in "The Protection of the Inept," *American Sociological Review* 32 [1967], 5–18); and Merton (in a private communication) has pointed to the distinction between obvious functional relations between sex and occupation (the occupation of wet nurse for example) and the relationship established between sex and occupation because of current statistical regularities in sex distribution.

The percentages of women in certain occupations[5] vary among Western countries (although they are consistently low), but they differ considerably from the percentages reported for the same occupations in the U.S.S.R. and Soviet-bloc countries. Women comprise 75 percent of the medical profession in the Soviet Union compared with 6 percent in the United States. The Russians identify medicine as a female occupation; Americans consider medicine a male occupation.

Sex Typing, Occupational Roles and Sex Roles

Because sex typing often incurs society's rationalizations about the male nature of some work and the female nature of other work (leading to such irrelevant fears as that women lawyers are masculine and that male home economists are effeminate), many occupations come to be viewed as extensions of a sex role. Cultures demand that one must do masculine work to be considered a man, and *not* do it to be a feminine woman.

These attitudes often have been legitimized in law. For example, in 1869, the U.S. Supreme Court upheld the Illinois State Bar's refusal to admit Mrs. Myra Bradwell with the observation that "the natural and proper timidity and delicacy which belong to the female sex evidently unfit it for many of the occupations of civil life." [6]

Though this particular decision was swept away long ago, some laws and many legal precedents rooted in the same sentiments have been retained for years, many until the passage of the 1964 Civil Rights Act. Attitudes, however, have proven even more difficult to change.

Because of sex-role associations in the United States, teaching, nursing, and social work have become female occupations, not only because of the statistical distribution of the sexes in them (two-thirds or more of each of these professions are staffed by women), but because they are said primarily to involve tasks

---

[5] See Tables 1–3 in Introduction, above.
[6] "The Perils of Portia," *Time* (March 6, 1964), p. 47.

judged to be "expressive" and person-oriented — helping, nurturing, and empathizing. Occupations believed to require qualities of coolness, detachment, analytic objectivity, or object-orientation, such as law (in which women have never constituted more than 3.5 percent of the profession) and engineering (in which women have never been more than 1 per cent) are male occupations. Thus, American society holds that women cannot be good engineers or lawyers because these professions call for qualities which are not feminine. We now know that these differences are not rooted in the female's biology. One need only look at the example of the Soviet Union where women are about one-third of the lawyers and engineers.[7] It is to be doubted that American women have many biological limitations not shared by their Russian sisters. And if biological difference is not the core, the definition of femininity for professional life must be sought elsewhere.

The professions of law, medicine, engineering, and teaching in higher education have remained almost unalterably defined as male in the United States. The proportions of women in them has remained small and the slight changes in these proportions are seen as even more insignificant when considered in the light of enlarged opportunities as legal barriers to education, training, and employment have been gradually lowered. One may well wonder why, since there have been changes in the sex typing of some occupations.

The history of the sex typing of certain occupations and professions would be an interesting study in itself. Some occupations became the domain of one sex early in their development. In the United States, nursing and social work became occupations largely staffed by women; law and medicine became the domains of men. Even within occupations some specialties and areas of concentration became sex-associated. Pediatrics and psychiatry are "female" specialties in medicine as domestic relations and trusts and estates are in the legal profession.

The sex division of labor has always been with us, although

[7] See Russian figures in Table 3, p. 12.

it has been more pronounced in some periods than in others. In the early days of the United States much of the work of the agrarian economy was shared by men and women. Of course, many tasks were sex-typed: men did the heavy physical labor while women did much of the household work. Men, however, performed work in the home, especially during the winters, and women were involved in a wide range of farm activities. With the industrial revolution, men left many of the household and home-shop tasks they formerly had performed and women lost the work of the farm but remained at home and continued to do the work of the household.[8] Thus, housework became an exclusively feminine domain while the male assumed other occupational roles.

The course of occupational sex typing has not been logically consistent; occupations have shifted in definition from male to female and vice versa and the definition has not always matched the reality, that is, women often do "man's work" and men do "women's work." Midwifery, for example, was traditionally a female job and the assistance of men at childbirth was considered a serious breach of modesty. Not until recent times, and mainly in the West, has delivery of the newborn become basically the work of the (mostly) male medical practitioner.[9] The profession has lost its former title (*midwifery*), together with its female sex-role definition.

Though the prejudices against men assisting in childbirth are now thought to be Victorian, other equally tenuous reasons for sex typing in the occupations are accepted without criticism. By and large these rationales are used to exclude women from the prestigious male occupations, though they act as well to limit men's entry into female professions.

There is social and historical evidence to indicate that there is far more flexibility to sex-role and occupational-role typing

[8] Arnold Rose, "The Adequacy of Women's Expectations for Adult Roles," *Social Forces* 30, No. 6 (October 1951), 69–70.

[9] Of course, since in the Soviet Union most doctors are women, obstetrics remains a female occupation there.

than is apparent from observing the proportion of each sex in any occupation at any one time. A few historical examples may illustrate the point.

In colonial and pioneer days, primary-school teaching was a male occupation, ostensibly because women did not have the necessary stamina of mind to educate the young. Only with the shortage of men during the Civil War [10] and the growing press for mass education did the demand for teachers require that women be recruited. Women eventually became predominant in teaching and this development was matched by a change in public attitude toward education as a suitably female prerogative. Perhaps, too, because the marriage rate was lower and single women were available, mobile, more docile and manipulable, and because they could be hired at a much lower price than the man whose family responsibility was acknowledged, the "old-maid school teacher" image emerged. As more women began to marry and as a growing grade-school population required more teachers, married women were permitted to teach. The occupational image has changed from that of the old-maid teacher to that of the female (marital status unspecified) teacher.[11] There is some indication the proportion of men in primary-school education is growing, and this should bring another shift in image. Some young men today are choosing jobs as teachers in the hope that they will be exempted from military service. The course and duration of the war in Vietnam may

[10] Women also left their homes to work as nurses and seamstresses who made the clothing and other articles required by the military. Esther Petersen points to the Civil War as a turning point in "Working Women," *Daedalus* (Spring 1964), p. 672.

[11] Education remains the major field of most women undergraduates; in addition, almost one-third of freshmen women in other fields shift to education by their senior year. See Davis, *Great Aspirations*. More than 40 percent of all degrees awarded to women are in education; "What Educated Women Want," *Newsweek* (June 13, 1966), pp. 68–75. Also, the typical college-graduate career-woman was a schoolteacher. Of all the former coeds in Havemann and West's national sample who at the time of study were working at a job instead of marriage, nearly three out of five — the exact figure was 59 percent — were working in the field of education; Havemann and West, *They Went to College*, p.74.

have important unanticipated consequences for the sex composition of the teaching profession.

A similar pattern is traceable in the secretarial field. Though
at one time male secretaries and typists were common, today
they are an anomaly. Only in conservative, all-male work cultures, such as are found in certain Wall Street law firms, are
male secretaries still to be found. Part of the answer may be the
proliferation of jobs in the white-collar sector of the economy,
where women provide a source of cheap, transferable, and non-
demanding labor. Yet it is still unclear why males have come to
be excluded from many lower-level white-collar jobs in which
there is no defined masculine or feminine characteristic.
Women may make better subordinates simply because they accept their position and do not aim higher.

Some spheres of work remain unaffected by sex typing. Jobs
as bank tellers, for instance, seem to be open to both men and
women, and it will be interesting to see whether new jobs
which have come about through scientific innovation (for example, computer technology) will provide opportunities without sex definition. One may expect that a number of them too
will become polarized.

There are also large differences in sex typing of jobs from
country to country. One rarely hears of an American woman
dentist, but 75 percent of the dentists in Denmark are women
and dentistry is considered a female profession in some South
American countries. Women account for only 1 per cent of the
profession in this country.

The array of differences in the sex identification of certain
professions in various countries, and the changes in the percentages of male-female participation through the years in any one
country, indicate that popular rationalizations about the appropriateness of an occupation for men or women are nothing but
post factum explanations. While in the United States women
are thought appropriately to be channeled into the so-called expressive professions but not the hard-headed instrumental pro-

fessions such as medicine, in the Soviet Union, for example, women are actually channeled into medicine because it is defined as a nurturant occupation. At the 1964 Bryn Mawr Conference on the Roles and Status of Women in the Soviet Union, Miss Ljudmila Kasatkina, a Russian exchange student, stated that women were advised to go into the medical profession because it was "easier" for them and fitted their predispositions and talents, because medicine is a humanitarian pursuit, and healing and human welfare are typically female concerns. Analysis of the professions in American society shows that service aspects are central to them[12] — and by this reasoning any profession would be "appropriately fitting" to the female role.

Sex typing (and its attendant assumptions) is taken for granted even by professional observers of human behavior. Some studies have implied that the sex division of labor within the professions is an expression of realistic adjustments to private and professional demands. Kosa and Coker[13] contend that certain sex and professional roles are more compatible than others, and that practitioners of the minority sex in a profession experience role conflict. Citing the example of the woman public-health doctor, they maintain that existing specialization in the medical profession offers an institutional setting for reducing role conflict and, accordingly, female physicians tend to select fields of practice where the sex and professional roles are compatible, such as pediatrics, psychiatry, and public health. Yet, following Kosa and Coker's analysis, while it is true that public health offers women stable hours of work, "liberation from the entrepreneurial role," and the possibility of part-time jobs, the explanation offered does not seem to be valid for all

[12] See Parsons, "The Professions and Social Structure," in *Essays in Sociological Theory*, pp. 34–49; Merton, *Some Thoughts on the Professions in American Society*; Goode, "Community Within a Community: The Professions," *American Sociological Review* 22 (1957), 195–200; Wilensky, "The Professionalization of Everyone?" *American Journal of Sociology* 70 (1964), 137–158.

[13] Kosa and Coker, "The Female Physician in Public Health: Conflict and Reconciliation of the Professional and Sex Roles," *Sociology and Social Research* 49 (April 1965), 295.

specialties, for the temperaments of all women, or even in its assessment of their role demands as mothers and wives.

For example, no specialty has more unscheduled demands on time than pediatrics; when not in the office the pediatrician is on call almost constantly to deal with emergency accidents, middle-of-the-night fevers, and the many illnesses of early childhood. Although it is true that pediatrics offers the shortest residency program (two years required), and thus might be attractive to the female medical student, child psychiatry demands one of the longest residencies, matched only by surgery, and yet a large percentage of women physicians choose this field.

The "relief" from building a practice which is supposed to be attractive to the female public-health doctor is apparently not sought by many women attorneys who enjoy having their own practices, complete with the problems of getting and keeping clients. Many women lawyers report that private practice offers benefits to the working mother which far outweigh the entrepreneurial demands involved. There are in medicine male-dominated specialties that would be ideal for the woman physician with a family. Ophthalmology, for instance, is a specialty not generally characterized by emergencies; patients are usually obtained through referrals from colleagues, and a practice easily can be limited or expanded according to what time is available. The same is true for otolaryngology, radiology, and plastic surgery. In fact, a good set of reasons can be found for women working in almost any specialty of medicine.[14]

Arbitrary and illogical sex typing is evident in the legal profession. The Legal Aid Society has been and still is a haven for women lawyers, although many who begin practice there leave it for other work. This semiwelfare agency typically handles a high proportion of family cases: desertion, abandonment, and juvenile problems. (Some officials have estimated these as high as 40 percent.) Not only have men avoided legal aid work be-

[14] Apart from the few remaining specialties requiring exceptional displays of strength, for example, orthopedics.

cause of the low salary it pays, but family law cases are believed
to be paralegal — more social work than legal work. This con-
trasts strongly with a comparable situation in medicine, where
the fledgling doctor, as intern and resident, provides professional services for social welfare cases and considers it valuable
training for later practice. But the "charity" cases of legal aid
work provide skills that have little transferability to the higher
paying and higher prestige fields of business and corporate law.

Thus, legal aid work has not typically been the first choice of
aggressive and ambitious male lawyers and in consequence has
been relatively open to women lawyers. (Of course, even in the
women's specialties in this male-dominated profession, there
are more men than women professionals.) The high proportion and visibility of women in the field have led to its definition as suitable for women. This suitability in part has been
legitimized by involvement in this area with family matters
and women and children clients. Yet, on close analysis, the
family matters which come up in legal aid work are hardly
within the social or even psychic framework of the average
middle-class woman lawyer. Although many of the offenders
helped by the agency are juveniles, their crimes are often acts
of violence and brutality far outside the range of what middle-
class people would consider ordinary deviance. Most male lawyers face nothing more brutal than tax, corporate, or real-estate
problems; at most they will deal with the gentlemanly crimes
of embezzlement or tax manipulation. The woman lawyer in
legal aid work has a far better chance of getting cases involving
child brutality, rape, murder, incest, torture, and bestiality —
the family problems of the courts. Similarly, women lawyers
who ascend to the bench are usually assigned to the family
court system and must mete out justice on the same kinds of
cases. Such are the family matters considered appropriate to the
talents and emotions of women.

A woman lawyer engaged in legal aid work recently commented to me that the emotional toll on the women lawyers
who staffed her office was severe because of the nature of the

cases they handled. One of the cases she had recently handled involved four preteenage boys (between 7 and 11 years of age) who were charged, as second offenders, with the rape of a five-year-old girl. The boys had dragged the girl and her young brother to an abandoned house and heated a hacksaw blade in a fire. They allegedly had held the blade to the brother's throat and told the sister they would kill the boy if she did not submit and keep silent. The girl finally confessed the incident some months later and a staff lawyer was called upon to defend one of the boys. That a woman, more than a man, should be expected to bring understanding, compassion, or some special knowledge of society to this kind of case is ridiculous.

It is clear that neither men nor women per se are especially suited by reason of sex, education, or social conditioning to handle such cases. Rather, one trained in psychology and sociology as well as law would be the likely candidate, regardless of sex. However, one might predict that such a social-science-oriented specialty would probably become a female province within the legal profession.

Sex Typing Reflects Sex Ranking

It has been pointed out that men's work, whatever it is, tends to be most highly regarded in most societies,[15] and that highly regarded work seems to be reserved for men. Men rank first in the ranking of the sexes and they get the first-ranking jobs. Women rank second and lowest and get the second- and lowest-ranking jobs. This may be viewed as a constitutive relationship of the stratification system.

Thus, in the occupational hierarchy of American society, males predominate in such high-ranking occupations as the established professions. The second-class rank of women is mirrored in their occupational distribution. (Even the adored woman is never placed on an occupational pedestal.)

---

[15] Goode's suggestion is that "whatever the strictly male tasks are, they are defined as more honorific"; W. J. Goode, *The Family*, p. 70.

Moreover, within male occupations or professions, specialties or subfields considered most appropriate for women tend to be less prestigious and less remunerative. Although they make up only 6 percent of the medical profession in the United States, women comprise 11.04 per cent[16] of the low-ranking specialty of psychiatry.[17] For her study of women in medicine some years ago, Josephine Williams interviewed male and female medical students about the specialties that they felt were particularly suited to men or women.[18] Both groups agreed on the ability of women to perform well in those professions which had lowest prestige among those interviewed, such as anaesthesiology, obstetrics, gynecology, and pediatrics. No figures exist on how many women lawyers are in the low-ranking specialty of matrimonial law, but it is widely be-

[16] Statistics on women physicians in the United States from the American Medical Women's Association, 1740 Broadway, New York (unpublished Research Committee report, 1966).

[17] Psychiatry ranked lowest when medical students were asked to describe their judgment of the relative standing assigned to medical fields by the profession of medicine in a study reported by Robert K. Merton, Samuel Bloom, and Natalie Rogoff (*Journal of Medical Education* 31 [August 1956], 564). Psychiatry also ranks seventh out of ten places in a ranking of net income of medical specialties (William N. Jeffers, "How the Specialties Compare Financially," *Medical Economics* 44 [February 6, 1967], 71). *The New York Times* reported that the appointment of a psychiatrist, Dr. Frederick C. Redlich, as dean of the Yale Medical School, was a sign that psychiatry was *gaining* prestige in the medical world. The leading medical schools have tended to choose their deans from the more organically oriented fields. The *Times* quoted Redlich's comment that "a generation ago, I'm sure Yale wouldn't have considered a psychiatrist for a dean. But now we are taken more seriously" (March 15, 1967, p. 50). Norman Zinberg dissects the bases for the low evaluation of psychiatry in "Psychiatry: A Professional Dilemma," *Daedalus* 92 (1963), 808–823. Large percentages of women doctors also are found in pediatrics (18.7) which ranks ninth in net income (next only to general practice) but which ranks a little higher in prestige according to the medical students' evaluation (fourth). Very few women are found in the specialties evaluated both high in prestige and income; only 1.1 percent of surgeons are women. The only other Western country for which data were available on specialization of women physicians was the Federal Republic of Germany, where few women specialize at all (63.6 percent are in general practice) and, of those specializing, the largest percentage (10.1 percent) are pediatricians; 1 percent are surgeons.

[18] Williams, "The Professional Status of Women in Medicine." See also Lopage, *Women in Medicine*.

lieved within the profession that the percentage is disproportionately high. In Jerome Carlin's study of 801 members of the
the New York Bar, only 1 percent said that matrimonial law was
a main area of practice.[19] In a University of Michigan Law
School study of woman law school graduates during the period
1956–1965, 50 percent of those engaged in legal work said they
performed domestic relations work, and 60 percent reported
they were engaged in trust and estate work (also among the
lower-ranking specialties). Thirteen percent of my New York
sample of women lawyers listed matrimonial work as their specialty, but many more in the study who had general practices
handled a considerable number of matrimonial cases. The proportion of men engaged in these activities was lower.[20]

Hubert O'Gorman suggests part of the reason for the relatively low prestige of matrimonial work is because lawyers believe matrimonial law "isn't really law." They are believed to
require a minimum of legal skill and to put a premium on
non-legal knowledge.[21] Jerome Carlin also discusses the generally low regard in which divorce practice is held in his study of
the Chicago Bar.[22]

There probably also is a relationship between a profession's
rank and the extent to which men or women are involved in it.
Those professions and specialties of which women constitute a
large percentage (such as social work or elementary school
teaching) and those with a female clientele (obstetrics or trusts
and estates) are less prestigious.

Sex Typing as a Sexual Control

All societies control the sexual behavior of their members; social stability depends on fixing responsibility for the new generation and assigning them their places. Stratification systems

[19] Carlin, *Lawyers' Ethics*, p. 12.
[20] White, "Women in the Law," *Michigan Law Review* 65 (1967), 1062. See
my dissertation "Women and Professional Careers: The Case of the Woman
Lawyer," p. 212.
[21] Hubert J. O'Gorman, *Lawyers and Matrimonial Cases*, pp. 107–108.
[22] Carlin, *Lawyers on Their Own*, p. 97.

rest on these controls. Even where romantic love is institutionalized as the basis for marriage, societies control the pools of el-
igibles and create conditions under which socially homoga-
mous marriages occur.[23] Anywhere that men and women are
together without supervision or control, the potential for a socially *un*acceptable love and/or sexual relationship is present.
The occupational sphere is certainly one of these potential trouble zones, and it seems probable that the sex typing of occupations has as one consequence the control of the meeting and
mating of men and women both before and after marriage.
The typing of a high proportion of occupations as either male
or female is not unrelated to the fact that sex typing guarantees
lower frequency of contact between the sexes.

In addition, because one always finds controls in the upper
strata stronger and more numerous, it is not surprising that the
highest stratum of occupations — the professions — is so
strongly sex typed. The threat to the marriages of men and
women who work in intimate contact with members of the opposite sex who are not their spouses probably contributes to and
is reinforced by cultural feeling about the inappropriateness of
women working in male fields and vice versa.

Consequences of Sex Typing on Women's Employment

The more nearly a profession is made up entirely of members of one sex, the less likely it is that it will change its sex
composition in the future and the more affected will be the performance of those few members who are not of that sex. Sex
typing tends to be a self-perpetuating process operating according to the dynamics of the self-fulfilling prophecy.[24]

As long as certain occupations are defined as male, women
who seek entry to them will be defined as social deviants and

[23] See Goode, "The Theoretical Importance of Love," *American Sociological Review* 24 (1959), 38–47.
[24] For an enunciation of the complexities and consequences of the self-fulfilling prophecy, see Merton, "The Self-Fulfilling Prophecy," pp. 421–436, in his *Social Theory and Social Structure*.

subjected to social sanctions. As a result, they will be less often motivated even to consider professions defined as incompatible with women's other roles. Women in these occupations will tend to be discouraged from seeking advancement when they perceive that the opportunity structure is limited for them. Thus, as Robert Merton has indicated, they often retreat[25] (that is, leave the occupation) or seek alternative roads to recognition, which for women usually lead outside the occupation to the family. By such actions, they accept the truth that the female status and the professional status are mutually exclusive. The sex typing of occupations as male provides an uncomfortable social context for the women in them.

[25] Merton's category of "retreatism" applies here only in the sense that women leave a social role; only in some cases do they manifest the accompanying attribute of apathy (unless one views the tired housewife syndrome as a response to retreatism). See "Social Structure and Anomie: Continuities" in his *Social Theory and Social Structure*, pp. 187–190. Women's retreat may also be viewed as a response to role strain. Thus they are "eliminating role relationships" utilizing a technique pointed to by Goode as one of a number of possible adaptations which can be made by ego in a conflict situation; Goode, "A Theory of Role Strain," *American Sociological Review* 25 (August 1960), 484. Women who leave law abridge their status set and this is akin to the abridgement of role sets the ego may use in articulation of the role set; Merton, "The Role Set," *British Journal of Sociology* 8 (June 1957), 117.

V
INSIDE PROFESSIONAL LIFE: INTERACTION PERFORMANCE, AND IMPEDIMENTS

PROFESSIONS share many of the characteristics of communities.[1] They tend toward homogeneity and exercise exclusionary practices which deter the participation of persons or groups who do not possess characteristics defined as appropriate. They are characterized by shared norms and attitudes, which make for and perpetuate informal relationships. The work of the profession depends greatly on mutual understanding among its practitioners, on common standards of behavior which permit them to control their sphere, and on the use of particularistic criteria without much intervention from the public or the state.[2] Since the preferred and prestigious profes-

[1] William J. Goode, "Community Within a Community: The Professions," *American Sociological Review* 22 (1957), 195–200; Robert K. Merton refers to them as "subcultures" in "Some Preliminaries to a Sociology of Medical Education," in *The Student Physician* (R. K. Merton, George G. Reader, M.D., and Patricia Kendall, eds.), pp. 71–79.

[2] This is what Etzioni labels "normative control." He notes that normative

sions are dominated by males, there is a tendency to assume that women do not share, or do not have the capacity to share, the common norms.

Women meet resistance in the professions at the point of recruitment. It is clear that they face discriminatory practices, such as law school and medical school quotas on the number of women applicants admitted, reluctance to grant fellowship aid, and denial of jobs on the basis of sex. But these processes are often subtle. *The Journal of Medical Education* reported in a study of applicants to medical schools in 1964–1965[3] that male and female applicants were accepted in equal proportions throughout the institutions surveyed. Carol Lopate notes in her book on women doctors[4] that the overt exclusion of women no longer is practiced by medical schools, but that the proportion of women seeking admission has remained low and constant. She suggests that prejudice against women still exists and is now motivated by the fear that at some future point this minority group might begin to apply in greater numbers. Her interviews with heads of medical schools indicated that they were reluctant to admit a much higher proportion of women students than they have at present (close to 8 per cent).

Women who do apply and are admitted to professional schools and jobs still face a professional context which makes their participation uncomfortable and high-level performance difficult.

The Protégé System

The protégé system is typical of many professions, especially in their upper reaches. It operates both to train personnel in

---

control is more dependent on personal qualities than other organizational modes. It also is based on shared symbols. This means recruits to normative organizations (professions are viewed here as sharing the structural properties of organizations) must be either heavily preselected or socialized to "fit in." Again, socialization is informal. See Amitai Etzioni, *A Comparative Analysis of Complex Organizations.*

[3] Davis G. Johnson, "The Study of Applicants, 1964–65," *Journal of Medical Education* 40, No. 11 (1965), 1026–1027.

[4] Carol Lopate, *Women in Medicine*, p. 71.

certain specialties and to assure continuity of leadership. The
fields in which it exists are marked by interplay between the
formal and informal relationships of the practitioners. At certain levels one must be "in" to learn the job. Becker and Strauss
point out that where this is so, "until a newcomer is accepted
he will not be taught crucial trade secrets," much less advance
in the field.[5]

The sponsor-protégé, or master-apprentice, relationship may
inhibit feminine advancement in the professions. The sponsor
is most likely to be a man and will tend to have mixed feelings,
among them a nagging sense of impending trouble, about accepting a woman as protégé. Although the professional man
might not object to a female assistant—he might even prefer
her—he cannot identify her (as he might a male assistant) as
someone who will eventually be his successor. He will usually
prefer a male candidate in the belief that the woman has less
commitment and will easily be deflected from her career by
marriage and children. This presumed lack of commitment is
troublesome in the relationship even if the woman is accepted
as an apprentice or a protégé. She may be under considerable
strain because the sponsor may be oblivious of her other role
demands. In addition, her other role partners—husband, father, child—may be suspicious or resentful of her loyalty to
and dependence on the sponsor. The sponsor's wife may also be
suspicious of the ties between the sponsor and his female
protégée.[6] Many professional men feel it is wiser to avoid this
kind of domestic trouble.

Even if she serves an apprenticeship, the woman faces serious
problems at the next step in her career if she does not get the
sponsor's support for entrée to the inner circles of the
profession — support that a male apprentice would expect as a
matter of course. The sponsor may exert less effort in pro-

[5] Becker and Strauss, "Careers, Personality, and Adult Socialization,"
American Journal of Sociology 62 (November 1956), pp. 253–263.
[6] See William J. Goode, "A Theory of Role Strain," *American Sociological
Review* 25 (August 1960), 487–490.

moting a woman for a career-line job. He may feel less responsibility for her career because he assumes she is not as dependent on a career as a man might be. The Ruth Benedict-Franz
Boas relationship in the Columbia University Anthropology
Department was a dramatic example of this situation. Boas
considered Ruth Benedict, the wife of Stanley Benedict, "amply
supported and with the obligation of a wife, [as] someone for
whose talents he must find work and a little money, someone
on whom he could not make extreme demands and for whom
he need not be responsible." Only later, when Ruth Benedict
separated from her husband and pressed for professional standing, did Boas get her an assistant professorship.[7]

Because of the woman's presumed lack of commitment and
drive, the sponsor may be reluctant to present her to colleagues
as a reliable candidate for their long-term enterprises. It is true,
however, that if a woman can enter into a protégé relationship
it may be more important for her than for a man, and that a
male sponsor may make an extra effort to promote the female
protégée because he is aware of the difficulties she is apt to face.
In fact, she may be able to rise or gain notice in a field only because she is a protégée, although this form of entrée is not typical or necessary for men.

We cannot specify the conditions under which one or the
other pattern will prevail. It is probably highly contingent on
the social structure of the discipline or specialty in which the
relationship arises, the personalities of the sponsor and
protégée, and, of course, the quality of the woman's talent as
well as her personality and physical attractiveness.

Placement offices in professional schools also act as part of
the filtering system for the professions. Women students applying to them are encouraged to enter the specialties where they
will presumably meet least opposition, but which also are pe-

[7] Margaret Mead (ed.), *Anthropologist at Work: The Writings of Ruth
Benedict*, pp. 342–343. The illustration is cited in Jessie Bernard, *Academic
Women*, pp. 105–106.

ripheral to entry into the profession's elite core. Women are, for example, encouraged to seek government jobs. It is said that they prefer them. And in fact women professionals do go into government service in far greater proportion to their numbers than men, as Table 9 shows. In this respect they are much like other minority groups, such as Negroes.

TABLE 9

Professional Workers in Selected Occupations in
Government Service, by Sex (U.S., 1960)

(percentages)

Dentists		Lawyers		Doctors		Engineers	
Male	Female	Male	Female	Male	Female	Male	Female
0.03	10.0	14.0	27.0	14.0	30.0	17.0	32.0

Source: Adapted from Table 21, U.S. Bureau of the Census, 1960. Subject Reports. *Occupational Characteristics*, Final Report PC(2)–7A, 1963, p. 277.

Government employment is usually based on universalistic criteria of evaluation. It offers recognition of skill, not who or what the candidate is. The professional person in government may take competitive examinations, for example, to improve his position and thus avoid the barriers of sex or race status. For certain women, the appeal of government service also lies in its regularity of schedule and the security of job tenure. The preference of women for government work tends to be an outgrowth of the prejudicial structure of the professions rather than the attraction of unique qualities of government work.

Women are deflected from the course to the professional apex even if they should surmount the initial obstacles to participation in the top levels of their profession. For example, few women become full members of the large Wall Street firms; to be admitted at all is a sign of achievement. Instead of finding jobs randomly in the specialties of elite firms, they are guided into specialties which are not considered important or honored and which do not usually lead to partnership. Men usually avoid the specialties that are offered to women.

The woman's later progress is inhibited by her lack of free access to fellow practitioners and peers, clubs and associations — the circle in which job opportunities are made known and informal recommendations are made. Hall documented the interdependence of career advancement and sponsorship [8] in medicine by specifying the channels whereby younger doctors of proper class and acceptable ethnic origin are absorbed into the inner fraternity. He noted that perpetuation of the coterie depends on a steady flow of suitable recruits.

These difficulties combine to create a further impediment for the female professional. The sponsor wants to minimize his risks in adopting recruits. And for the group, an unsuitable member weakens its intimacy and solidarity. Thus the group may exert pressure on the sponsor to pick a protégé with whom it will be comfortable. "Hiring partners" in large law firms often claim their colleagues will laugh at them if they suggest bringing a young woman into the firm.

Finally, it may well be unwise for the sponsor to depend on a woman to continue to work as a male disciple might, or to assume that the work of a woman would be given serious attention. It is believed, for example, that women have not matched men in volume or excellence of scientific contributions. Few have attained positions of leadership or eminence which might have given their work wide exposure and visibility. A recent study of women Ph.D.'s [9] indicates that women match their male associates in productivity, the married women and those with children often doing more than the men or unmarried women (although they fail to receive as many grants as men). Two other studies, however, indicate that women do not al-

[8] Oswald Hall, cited in Becker and Strauss, *op. cit.*, p. 254. See also Amitai Etzioni's description of the way in which professional networks control information about professionals which establish their reputations as well as the limits of this control; Etzioni, *op. cit.*, p. 260.

[9] Rita James Simon, Shirley Merritt Clark, and Kathleen Galway, "The Woman Ph.D.," *Social Problems* 15 (Fall 1967), 221–236.

ways measure up to men. Maccoby's 1956 study of 400 Radcliffe Ph.D.'s showed that the women had a consistently lower rate of productivity than men, independent of their marital status.[10] A later study by Bernard compared several hundred female and male scientists and found that sex differences in productivity were insignificant at various levels of the academic hierarchy but that women tended to hold less productive positions.[11]

Whether or not there are real differences in productivity, it is certainly believed by both women and men alike that women do not produce equally. That belief has considerable power in excluding women from positions where productivity is important.

Informal Interaction — The Club Context

As noted earlier, interaction in the professions, especially in their top echelons, is characterized by a high degree of informality, much of it in an exclusive, clublike context.

It is difficult for someone not equipped with a set of appropriate statuses to enter this exclusive society and participate in its informal interactions, to understand the unstated norms, and to be included in the club's casual exchanges.[12] Exclusion may occur at any point in the career of the person possessing a wrong status. New York attorney Doris Sassower, President of the New York Women's Bar Association, recently reminded her membership of the bitter experiences of Florence Allen, Chief Judge of the U.S. Court of Appeals, Sixth Circuit, who could barely do her work when first appointed a federal judge.[13] The resistance of her fellow (male) judges was so

[10] Eleanor Maccoby (ed.), "Sex Differences in Intellectual Functioning," in *The Development of Sex Differences*, pp. 25–55.

[11] Bernard, *op. cit.*, pp. 160–170. Professor Bernard also reviews a number of studies of productivity and finds that generally women's output is lower than men's although sometimes the differences are negligible.

[12] Erving Goffman, in *Stigma*, points out that failure to sustain the many minor norms important in the etiquette of face-to-face communication can have a very pervasive effect on a person's acceptability in social situations.

[13] Speech at the Waldorf-Astoria Hotel, May 13, 1967, on the occasion of the first Florence E. Allen Award.

great that they refused to speak to her or to look at her except when absolutely forced to by the business at hand.

In many professions, men have chosen to conduct their business in men's faculty and university clubs, men's bars, golf and athletic clubs, and during poker games. In addition, many once informal traditions have developed into rigidly formalized male cults, as, for example, the academic "high table" in the colleges of Cambridge and Oxford. Obstacles abound not only for females aspiring to membership in such groups, but also for males from an alien social class or social tradition. Informal systems of introduction and support abound in the job markets of many countries (Mexico and Israel are two), but not in the United States and other nations where technical skills count most. In the United States, ability and achievement alone may only occasionally suffice to insure a good career; the talented but retiring and the promising but nonconforming may simply fall by the wayside.

The only possible antidote for the familiarity and lineage which oil the wheels in professional environments is power through rank, seniority, money, or charisma; women do not often have any of these defenses.

As we have seen, professionals group in informal networks to have access to the established knowledge of their professions. This is also true in the acquisition of new knowledge. Sir Alfred Egerton has noted that, in the fast-moving sciences, "Of the total information extant, only part is in the literature. Much of it is stored in the many brains of scientists and technologists. We are as dependent on biological storage as on mechanical or library storage." [14] Access to this source of information — the brains of fellow scientists — may be more limited for women than for men, for evidence suggests that women are not involved in professional networks to the extent that men are.[15] Bernard's study of women zoologists showed that women faculty members at colleges had less contact with fellow scientists

[14] Cited in Bernard, *op. cit.*, p. 303.
[15] *Ibid.*, p. 152.

than did men. They were less likely than other scientists to attend meetings of professional societies. They were also less likely than male scientists to be on regular mailing lists for reprints of research articles. Women on the staffs of universities seemed to do better in becoming part of the communication network, but this was not true of women in the social sciences. Sylvia Fleis Fava reported that, in 1952, although women constituted 14.6 percent of all professionally employed sociologists, they constituted only about 9 percent of those participating in annual professional meetings.[16] This may suggest that women are less likely to succeed in fields which require the professional to operate as one of a team of equals rather than alone. This may account for the fact that society recognizes more famous women artists than women lawyers, more women pianists than orchestra conductors, more women writers than women surgeons.[17] Of course, as some women gain eminence, the problem diminishes or disappears for them. A Van Cliburn may study with a gifted and established pianist like Rosina Lhévinne without the issue of male-female superiority ever arising, and it is improbable that Anna Freud or Karen Horney were ever rejected as training analysts by younger male psychoanalysts.

Eminence also often correlates with age, which may further reduce the focus placed on sex status. Many of the feminine role components attached to the female sex status become less intrusive in interactions between men and women as the woman grows older; it is probably accurate to suppose that in most cases as the woman ages, her sexual appeal becomes less an object of focus. Since a woman is apt to encounter resistance if her professional status requires the exercise of authority over

[16] Sylvia Fleis Fava, "The Status of Women in Professional Sociology," *American Sociological Review* 25 (1960), 271–272.

[17] Even holding constant the fact that there *are* more women artists, pianists, and writers than women lawyers, orchestra conductors, or surgeons, women in the latter occupations are hardly ever mentioned, for example, by the *New York Times*, or *Time*, which I have examined for the past four years for items about women in top positions.

others, she may find that she can depend on deriving a certain amount of authority from her age. While a man might resent "taking orders" from a woman, he probably would be less resistant if the woman is older. Thus, the woman needs not only the rank which derives from her status as an expert, but also that from her age status. Correlatively, when the woman is younger than the man, or the same age, she is more apt to encounter resistance to her authority.

Self-Exclusion by Professional Women

In many cases, men do not actively exclude women; the women themselves limit interaction. Although there might be a rebuff if the woman initiated contact, the situation is often never put to the test. In Jessie Bernard's study of scientists, the women surveyed were less aggressive than the men in actively seeking formal communication, even by mail, although they took advantage of opportunities offered to them about as much as the men. These self-imposed limitations on interaction [18] within occupational frameworks are another example of the self-fulfilling prophecy that leads the woman toward unnecessary career limitations and, sometimes, failure.

Some of the women lawyers I interviewed, for example, avoided joining colleagues at lunch. One commented, "Sometimes when the natural thing to do would be to join an associate and a client at lunch if you were a man, you feel, well, maybe I'd better not. It might be awkward for them. They might want to talk about something and might feel constrained."

This behavior results largely from the image of a profession as a society of men, an image many male practitioners would like to perpetuate. Men accomplish this most effectively by convincing the woman that she does not belong and should not want to belong. Most women get the message, and for those who don't there are the explicit devices of separate women's en-

[18] Bernard, *op. cit.*, p. 159.

trances to clubs normally limited to male members and restaurants limited to male patronage during lunch hours. Of course there is no shortage of places for male and female colleagues to lunch together, but many men seem to favor the club setting and when women go along they go through "the back entrance." The separate "white" and "colored" doors to public places in the recent past were condemned as unjust and demeaning to black people by many persons who feel that separate women's entrances are part of an acceptable tradition.

Not only do women exclude themselves, but they often favor the exclusion of other women. They accept the image of the male profession and its male-specific behavior. The more informal the professional context, the more willing women seem to concede the rightness of their exclusion. One woman lawyer interviewed described her feelings about the day when she was the only woman who went to meetings of a local bar association: "There was a camaraderie in the County [Law] Association — a terrific spirit. In other associations the members are very staid . . . but there everybody knows one another and they joke. They were prejudiced against admitting women but I think they were justified. It's not the same with a woman around. They aren't free to express themselves, to tell off-color stories — they should have that."

This attitude persists in spite of the fact that many valuable professional contacts and referrals of cases are made in these informal situations. The exclusivity perpetuated by the male leaders of the legal profession in New York City is illustrated by the fact that the county bar associations of Brooklyn and Queens counties have only recently admitted women to membership, thirty years after the city's larger, more prestigious, and more formal bar associations — the New York County Lawyers' Association and the Association of the Bar of the City of New York — admitted women.[19]

[19] This may seem like a contradiction of the principle that exclusivity is most pronounced at the top echelons of professions. But in informal situations

Problems of Conforming to Professional Norms

Women often do not act as good professionals and thus their career involvement and advancement are limited. In this respect they share problems with others who have deviant status. These problems are complex in the professional context, but they mirrored clearly by the woman's performance.

PROPORTION OF CONTRIBUTIONS

Women in male-dominated professions probably make proportionately fewer contributions to their professions than do men. The definition of "contribution" varies from field to field, and a full-scale study of the problem has yet to be made. But few women achieve fame for discoveries in science[20] or are known for prodigious writing. Since 1901, only five women have won Nobel prizes in science, although Marie Curie received both physics (1903) and chemistry (1911) prizes. Her daughter, Irène Joliot-Curie, attained the prize in 1935 for her discovery, with her husband, of artificial radioactivity; Gerty Cori won the Nobel prize for medicine in 1947; Maria Mayer won the Nobel award in physics for her work on the nuclear shell model (1963) and Dorothy Hodgkin was a prize winner in chemistry (1964).

Even in the Soviet Union, where women constitute a large

---

there is less of a span between the general membership and the elite corps. The high-ranking associations let women in but keep them low in the hierarchy.

[20] There were almost no eminent women scientists, for example, before the nineteenth century and few after. Cora Castle, in *A Statistical Study of Eminent Women*, found twenty women eminent as scholars from between the 7th century B.C. and the end of the 19th century A.D. Among them were Hypatia, the mathematician, 5th century A.D.; the Abbess Hildegard, physicist and doctor, 12th century A.D.; and Caroline Herschel, who discovered a number of comets in the 18th century. Mabel Newcomer in *A Century of Higher Education for Women*, made a study of *American Men of Science* for the year 1946 in which women made up 7 percent of the entries but only 3 percent of the starred entries (distinguished scholars). Both works are cited in Patricia Frithiof, "Women in Science" (Lund, Sweden: University of Lund, November 1967), mimeographed.

proportion of all professions, the chances are few that they will be well represented among the eminent.[21] Dodge points out that the discrepancy between the sexes in the U.S.S.R. is greatest at the highest levels of scholarly achievement. No women are to be found in the upper levels of the Academy of Sciences of the U.S.S.R., and only a few among the full and corresponding members of the academy. Few women have won the Lenin Prize and typically they have been members of sizable research teams.

If publication is used as a criterion, it is probably true that women are responsible for proportionately fewer books or articles recognized as important in the professions. There is contradictory evidence, however, as to whether or not they publish adequately at all. In sociology, women contributed less than 10 percent of the articles published in the *American Sociological Review* and presented fewer than 9 percent of the papers presented at annual meetings of the American Sociological Association during the years 1949-1958.[22] In 1966, when women constituted about 15 percent of professionals in the fied of sociology, they presented less than 7 percent of the papers at the annual meeting of the ASA.[23] Dodge notes that Soviet women make a good showing as contributors of scholarly articles but that their contributions have been only about half as large as their numbers would suggest.[24] The Simon research [25] shows that if year and field are held constant, American women Ph.D.'s publish as much as their male colleagues, and married women Ph.D.'s publish slightly more. This is certainly not the impression most members of the academic profession, both male and female, have of the women in their midst. It is clear that, what-

[21] Norton Dodge, *Women in the Soviet Economy*, pp. 227–237.

[22] Fava, *op. cit.*, p. 272.

[23] Computed from data in *American Science Manpower*, 1964, National Science Foundation, NSF 66–29. (Washington, D.C.: U.S. Government Printing Office.)

[24] Dodge, *op. cit.*

[25] Simon, Clark, and Galway, *op. cit.*, pp. 221–236.

ever the reality or rate of female participation, the visibility of the contributions is low. None of these consequences are the result of any plot to suppress the work of women. They are, again, an outgrowth of the network and climate of the major professions.

VISIBILITY OF CONTRIBUTIONS

Work performed at the larger and more prestigious institutions probably has a greater chance of attracting notice than work which comes out of lesser known institutions. It is hard to know which comes first: Do women tend to cluster in less prestigious institutions in part because they publish less than men, or does their failure to win posts at high-prestige institutions cut them off from the culture in which publishing is encouraged? In any case, publishing and association with a top quality institution seem to be related.

The halo effect of the institution can be important to the author whose identity is not commonly known. Readers scanning a journal might read an article by an unknown academic when he is affiliated with a prestigious university but skip the work of an unknown at a low-ranking college or university.[26]

In 1963, 82 percent of women faculty members, compared with 74 percent of the men, worked in colleges and technical institutions with faculties numbering under 200. Women faculty members were also affiliated with smaller universities to a greater extent than were men; 37 percent of the women, compared with 43 percent of the men were in institutions with over 750 faculty members.[27] In law, few women are in large firms or serve as judges in superior courts. None has ever held a position on the U.S. Supreme Court.

[26] Steven Cole and Jonathan R. Cole have found that the visibility of physicists, for example, is highly correlated with the rank of the department in which they work; "The Visibility and the Structural Bases of Awareness of Scientific Research," *American Sociological Review* 33 (June 1968), 397–413.

[27] Ralph E. Dunham, Patricia D. Wright, Majorie O. Chandler (Higher Education Studies Branch), "Teaching Faculty in Universities and Four-Year Colleges," pp. 64–65.

Contributions are made visible by the support of senior men in the field or by joint publications with those in eminent positions.[28] We tentatively suppose that women's contributions are not promoted equally with men's and that women less often collaborate with those in eminent positions.

On the other hand, women professionals in male-dominated professions have greater visibility than men simply because they are a minority. They are physically more visible (as are Negroes) at professional meetings and in other professional encounters, and their names identify their sex in their written work.[29] When their work is good, it may get even greater notice than that of men who perform at the same level of competence. If they perform badly, the same is unfortunately true; they will stand out.

Merton has observed that under certain circumstances ideas or discoveries "fall on deaf ears" if they are not promoted by an "acceptable" person. Professional women report reluctance to engage in activities that might be defined as self-promotional.[30] There seem to be two major reasons for this. First, they define assertiveness as inappropriate to their feminine role and, second, they tend to feel less of a need to promote themselves than do men, because they are not as ambitious. Women professionals tend to be more satisfied with their place in professions and do not feel it necessary to press for the attention that will guarantee advancement.

Further, the woman's sex status may create enough "noise" to drown out what she has to say. Psychological studies suggest

[28] Zuckerman finds, for example, that Nobel laureates who themselves had laureate masters received the prize, on the average, nine years earlier than scientists who had not studied with a prizewinner: Harriet Zuckerman, "Nobel Laureates in Science: Patterns of Productivity, Collaboration, and Authorship," *American Sociological Review* 32 (1967), 393.

[29] Zuckerman has brought to my attention the fact that, until a few years ago, in psychology journals initials only were used for men's given names but women's names were spelled out in full.

[30] In informal interviews conducted in the early stages of this study with women in academic life, science, law, and medicine. Some tend to be bitter that they are not recognized but still are loath to press for recognition.

that both men and women tend to attach less importance to information from a female colleague. Here the sex status intrudes in the dynamics of professional interaction and communication in a way similar to the reaction faced by one who has made discoveries in a field other than his own. The outsider's inappropriate status ("inappropriate" in the same sense that the woman's status is) makes people in the field resistant to the finding or supercautious in evaluating it.[31] One eminent woman judge interviewed for my study of women lawyers[32] complained that in her three decades of experience in law she had learned that men "just haven't got the habit" of listening to a woman, even if she was acknowledged to be "smart and adroit," unless they wanted specific information from her. The main problem, the judge said, was in getting male colleagues to engage in a general exchange of ideas. Other women lawyers believed their word carried weight in professional interactions once their competence had been established. Lopate reports that female interns often face resistance on the part of patients in accepting diagnoses of their illness. Patients don't believe they are seeing "the doctor," when they see a woman.[33]

TIME DEVOTED TO THE PROFESSION

Women professionals work fewer hours than male colleagues. Although styles of work differ, the true professional's involvement with his field is expressed in the long hours he puts in. Women in the professions do not devote to their work the same number of hours as their male counterparts. Although the mean number of work hours reported in census figures for women in the male-dominated professions was between 35 and 39 hours per week (a figure which includes work hours re-

[31] In science, the classic case is, of course, Louis Pasteur, who met violent resistance from the medical men in advancing his germ theory because he was a chemist. See Bernard Barber's observation on professional specialization being a cause of resistance to discovery in "Resistance by Scientists to Scientific Discovery" in B. Barber and W. Hirsh (eds.), *The Sociology of Science*, pp. 539–556.

[32] Dissertation.

[33] Lopate, *op. cit.*, p. 114.

ported by women working part-time), this is less than the 37-to 47-hour average work week reported for male professionals.[34] One problem faced by professional women is that "full-time" work is usually not considered an adequate commitment for the professional person, who is expected to put in many more hours than the average worker in another occupation. Women who confine their professional activity to a normal 35-hour week are not conforming to professional norms. Furthermore, many women professionals work part-time, an option not open to a man who must support a family but whose dedication to his work might not even be as great as the woman's. The lower number of hours women work in the professions has many consequences for their visibility, their inclusion in formal responsibilities and informal networks, and the kinds of specialties and areas of work they may select.[35] All of these consequences place them in a disadvantageous position in professional life.

INVOLVEMENT

Women are less involved in professional organizations. Membership and participation in professional organizations is typical and expected of the active professional. It is, indeed, generally believed that fewer women than men join professional associations. Studies done by Sylvia Fava[36] and Jessie Bernard[37] on sociologists and zoologists, respectively, support this, but there is evidence that the generalization is a myth. In her study of women Ph.D.'s,[38] Simon found that 90 percent of the women in her sample (both married and unmarried), as well as 90 percent of the male Ph.D.'s, belonged to at least one professional organization. Membership of women lawyers in

[34] See Table 9, p. 184, for a comparison of mean numbers of hours reported for men and women in the scientific and technological professions and in law. Jeanette Johansson has pointed out to me that women in some specialties of engineering are restricted by law to a 35- to 37-hour week in some states.
[35] For a discussion of these consequences for women lawyers, see my dissertation, pp. 302–324.
[36] Fava, op. cit., pp. 171–172.
[37] Bernard, op. cit., p. 152.
[38] Simon, Clark, and Galway, op. cit., p. 234.

TABLE 10

Weekly Hours of Employed Lawyers, Engineers, Scientists, and Technicians, by Sex
(U.S., 1960)

Occupation	Hours (mean)		Hours worked (percentage)					
			Men			Women		
	Men	Women	1–34	35–40	41+	1–34	35–40	41+
Lawyers and judges	46.7	38.9	6	33	59	22	47	28
Engineers	42.8	38.6	1	67	32	9	82	9
Scientists	42.1	38.6	5	68	27	11	75	14
Biologists	43.0	39.1	6	58	36	12	66	21
Chemists	41.6	38.8	4	72	24	9	80	11
Mathematicians	41.4	38.6	3	74	23	6	87	7
Physicists	41.6	(a)	5	72	23	18	59	23
Technicians:								
Medical and dental	42.2	38.5	10	51	39	15	61	24
Electrical and electronic	42.2	39.8	3	70	27	5	81	14
Other engineering and physical-science technicians	41.5	38.7	4	71	25	8	80	12
Professors-Instructors:								
Biological sciences	43.6	33.8	17	28	54	37	28	35
Chemistry	40.8	(a)	25	25	50	41	26	33
Engineering	42.5	(a)	15	32	53	60	20	20
Mathematics	36.4	35.4	34	30	36	37	31	32
Physics	40.5	(a)	26	26	48	54	—	46

Source: U.S. Bureau of the Census, Census of Population, 1960. Subject Reports. *Occupational Characteristics*, Final Report PC (2)–7A, 1963, Table 13.

a Mean not shown when case base less than 1,000.

bar associations is about equal to their membership in the profession of law as a whole; they make up about 3 percent of the
profession and about 3 percent of the members of both national
and local bar associations in New York City, for example.[39]

However, it is no myth that in times past women's participation in professional organizations has been low; if today it approaches the level of male participation, there is a significant
change from the pattern of the past.

Some of women's reticence to participate in professional
organizations is due to unconcealed discrimination by these
groups in the past, the recent past in some cases. Where there
were no legal barriers based on sex (or where these were removed), women were excluded on other grounds or by informal means. In New York City, both the Brooklyn Bar Association and the Bronx Bar Association avoided the equality issue,
barring women with the excuse that no rest-room facilities
were available for them.[40] (It is interesting that the same excuse was employed by Cambridge and Oxford universities to
limit enrollment of women [41] and by the Princeton University
Graduate School. This particularly courageous stand has probably been widely used to bar women.)

Although no professional organizations today exclude
women, admission has not generally taken the form of enthu-
siastic invitation. Women have not been permitted full participation at decision-making levels, and they are seldom elected to
important committees or to executive posts.

In psychology, and psychiatry, fields popularly considered to
be within women's scope of interest and competence, women
have remained singularly unrecognized by the professional as-

---

[39] Figures for 1966–1967 computed from membership directories of the New
York County Lawyers' Association and the Association of the Bar of the City
of New York. For further analysis of lawyers' role in professional organizations, see my dissertation, pp. 278–301.

[40] Reported to me by several members of the Brooklyn Bar.

[41] David Caute, "Crisis in All Souls," *Encounter* 26 (1966), 5. Women,
however, were accorded the full status of members of the university at Oxford
in 1920 and at Cambridge in 1948 (*Education in Britain*, revised edition,
British Information Service, January 1964, p. 8).

sociation. Mitchell reported in 1951 [42] that women had not become fellows, officers, committee chairmen, committee members, editors, representatives to other organizations, members of the Council of Representatives, members-at-large, members of the Executive Committee, or division presidents of the American Psychological Association in proportion to their numbers and qualifications. In 1968 no women held major offices, although they were represented on the board of directors. Only as secretaries have they served in proportion to their numbers.

In sociology, of the fifty-six presidents of the American Sociological Association elected to date (1968), only one has been a woman (Dorothy Swaine Thomas).

In law, no women have ever served as presidents of the national bar associations or the important local associations. Within the bar associations women tend to serve disproportionately on such low-ranking committees as those involving family law,[43] though this reflects their higher representation in the specialties of matrimonial and family law for the reasons discussed earlier. For example, in a listing of the principal committees and members of the New York County Lawyers' Association for 1967-1968, women were members of fourteen of the association's thirty-seven committees. In only four instances were there more than two women on a committee: Children and Youth and the Courts (five of sixteen members); Law, Psychology and Psychiatry (eight of sixteen); Family Court (six of sixteen); and Surrogates Court (three of twenty-three members). No woman was listed as chairman of any committee. Of a total of 1,103 members of the State Bar of California serving on committees, only eighteen are women.[44] Of course, these figures do not reflect the dynamics of participation. Probably many or most male members of professional associations

[42] Mildred B. Mitchell, "Status of Women in the American Psychological Association," *American Psychologist* 6 (1951), 200.

[43] *New York Times* (August 6, 1967), p. 37.

[44] Letter from Karl E. Zellman, Assistant Secretary, State Bar of California, March 21, 1967.

are not active in them because they have no time or interest to do so. It is probable that the active women participants are even more committed than the active males because typically they must make a special effort to fit such participation into their schedules. Simon's study of Ph.D.'s finds that the unmarried women seem to have higher participation rates than other women or the men, because most male professionals tend to be married and, of course, have responsibilities at home and wish to spend time with their families.[45] It is probably true that committed women of top rank in the professions cannot and do not participate in their associations to the extent that the top men do.

To some extent, the establishment of parallel women's organizations has served to deflect women's participation in professional groups. In some professions, women's organizations were established in response to the extreme discrimination against them [46] and others as special-interest groups. The separate women's organizations deplete the pool of potential female leadership in the major professional organizations and siphon off the energy of women members, especially where the women's group attempts to duplicate the functions of the major (integrated) group. Women's groups usually have continued to exist even after women have been permitted to join the men's organizations. The separate groups meet some of the unique needs of women in professional life. They serve as friendship

[45] Simon, Clark, and Galway, *op. cit.*

[46] For example, the National Council of Women Psychologists was established in 1942 after it became clear that the Emergency Committee in Psychology of the National Research Council was continuing to omit women from its plans for the wartime use of psychologists; Mitchell, *op. cit.*, p. 193. The National Association of Women Lawyers was founded in 1899. Local women's bar associations in New York were also formed in response to exclusion by the men in the Bronx, Queens, and Brooklyn. There are also separate professional associations for women in medicine (founded 1915), dentistry (founded 1921), geography (founded 1925), certified public accounting (founded 1933) and engineering (founded 1950). In professions typed as female, there are no separate men's organizations, nor have men been legally excluded from membership at any time.

groups and centers for mutual support in a sometimes hostile professional world. They act as clearing houses for contacts and clients in much the same way as the male-dominated associations serve their male colleagues. Further, ideas and information can be exchanged among colleagues in the women's associations without intrusion of the sexual component. Women also report that it is easier to question a female colleague on a point of information, because asking a male colleague might reinforce the male view of women as incompetents.

Women blocked from rising in the male-dominated professional associations can climb to positions of leadership in the parallel organizations. Although the prestige attached to high position in a woman's organization ranks much lower than that of a comparable position in the male-dominated group, some women do, at least, become visible to the profession by their activity within the female sector.

The younger female professionals generally consider women's groups (of any kind) as vestigial structures of a bygone period. The continuing expression of this attitude may well constitute a death sentence for professional women's organizations. Without young recruits, the separate organizations will probably become extinct and women will move toward greater involvement in the major professional societies.

Differential Placement in the Professional Structure

Fewer women hold high-ranking jobs not only because of overt discrimination and exclusion, but because their sex status places them disadvantageously in the structure of the profession. Many of the reasons previously stated for their failure to be recognized for professional contributions apply here.

They are routed into less visible positions — the background, backroom jobs — where their performance may not come to the attention of superiors or the public. Women tend to be given library research and are less likely to work directly with the client.

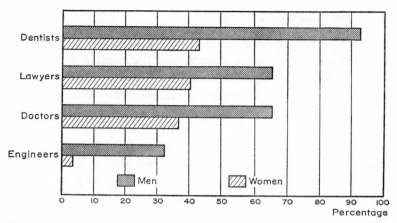

Figure 1. Self-Employed Men and Women, Selected Professions. (*Adapted from Table 21, U.S. Bureau of the Census; 1960 Subject Reports, Occupational Characteristics, Final Report PC(2)-7A, 1963, p. 277.*)

The specialties in which they predominate are typically regarded as the less important and less demanding ones. Even if they should demonstrate skill in these specialties, it counts for less.

The specialties in which they predominate are less lucrative. Women lawyers in a relatively unprofitable specialty, such as matrimonial law, are less apt to gain distinction and to advance in better firms because they are unable to contribute substantially to the firm's total profits. This is probably true also for women engineers and architects. Women are also seldom given important clients; their comparatively unimportant clients cannot effectively press for their promotion.[47]

Women tend less than men to be in positions where they can exercise much autonomy. Those who work in the male-dominated professions are self-employed (see Figure 1) to a far lesser degree than are men. They are also less likely to be in decision-making positions if they are on the staffs of institutions or in professional or business firms.

[47] See Erwin Smigel's evaluation of client sponsorship as a path to partnership in a large firm in *The Wall Street Lawyer*, pp. 100–102.

The Interactional Setting

Performance of the professional task may be seriously affected when colleagues, clients, and the woman professional focus on her sex status and not her occupational status. An example of this is the patient whose response to a woman doctor is to flirt with her and to feel uneasy about revealing his ailments (because it would be "unmanly"). Responses directed at her sex status color both the attitudes and the behavior of the woman practitioner. Consequences result which may stand in the way of professional performance, although to a limited extent they may be turned to her advantage.

SELF-CONSCIOUS REACTIONS OF THE WOMAN

Focus on sex status usually marks the start of each new professional encounter of the woman professional. She is thus often made self-conscious and unsure whether she will be received with surprise and whether the reception will be favorable. Women professionals face the same situation as other individuals who have a highly visible trait or status.[48] The woman is like a "stigmatized" person (as Goffman points out) who feels he is "on," "having to be self-conscious and calculating about the impressions he is making, to a degree and in areas of conduct where he assumes others are not."[49]

Women cannot rely on normal cues to make things easier.[50]

---

[48] A young Negro lawyer recently recalled his first case, in which he was called upon to defend a burglar. The thief, white, appeared before the judge dressed as he had been when apprehended by the police, in dirty work clothes, his hair mussed, an unshaven face. The lawyer, of course, was neatly dressed in a business suit, was well shaven, and was carrying a briefcase. The judge looked at both men and asked, unjokingly, "Which man is the lawyer?" He clearly was unable to visualize what a Negro lawyer should look like.

[49] Goffman, *Stigma*, pp. 13–14, 33.

[50] This problem is identified by Barker, who points to the uncertainty of status for the disabled person in a wide range of social interactions, including employment. "The blind, the ill, the deaf, the cripples, can never be sure what the attitude of a new acquaintance will be, whether it will be rejective or accepting, until the contact has been made. This is exactly the position of the adolescent, the light-skinned Negro, the second generation immigrant, the socially mobile person and the woman who has entered a predominantly mas-

During my interviews with women lawyers, for example, some recalled being taken for secretaries when they went to a new courtroom, and reported searching for ways to communicate to male attorneys that they were colleagues and wished to be treated in a professional manner. Women physicians are often faced with similar problems when they present themselves as doctors in a clinic or a hospital ward where the patients have not been forewarned of their sex status, cued by the doctor's nameplate on her office or by an introduction. Students in universities are often surprised when a female instructor appears, especially if she is young and attractive. The woman professional must often brusquely impose her professional status on an interaction to keep the role partner from violating the norms of professional relationship.

For the woman professional, the working environment is always transmitting messages that she is unique, and she anticipates them. She may easily become paranoid. Some women overact and attempt to conceal or inhibit "womanly attributes"; they are cold instead of exhibiting warmth and charm, or they dress in severely tailored clothes (a pattern which is, however, more representative of a generation now in retirement). More common is the propensity of some women to overconform or overproduce in an attempt to make up for their downgraded status.

PROVING THEMSELVES

Women in professions often asserted, during interviews, that they spent more time on work than a man would because they "must be better than a man." One woman expressed the feeling vividly: ". . . if you're a woman, you have to make less mistakes. . . . a woman must put greater effort into her work . . . because if you make a fool of yourself, you're a damn fool woman instead of just a damn fool." Some women try to win male colleagues or clients over by using their femi-

---

culine occupation"; "The Social Psychology of Physical Disability," *Journal of Social Issues* 4 (1948), 34.

nine qualities to advance toward the professional goal. They admit to flirting to attract attention or to persuade when the dispassionate approach fails. It is clear that most women in professional life disapprove of this, even though they may use it from time to time. All seem to agree that it is worth nothing unless backed up with a superior performance, command of the subject, and skill. They are all conscious of a special need to prove themselves and agree that this need continues throughout the professional career. Such an attitude, and its attendant compulsive behavior and overconformity reactions, are typical of strivers in blocked opportunity structures.[51] Women try to fulfill professional task norms even if they do not have access to the means available to men, who alone have the correct sex status in the professional context.

BEING UNOBTRUSIVE

Women may also try to be as unobtrusive as possible,[52] and not attract attention ("create trouble"), by holding back in conversation or by accepting work which keeps them in invisible positions, such as library work or government work in which they do not have individual clients.[53] This unobtrusiveness is a reflection of women's position within the informal structure of the profession. Women are sensitive to men's desire to be left to their own company and feel that their presence would interfere with the "normal" functioning of things; they sometimes fear also that their friendliness will be misinterpreted as being sex-

[51] These two types of behavior are identified by Merton in "Social Structure and Anomie," in *Social Theory and Social Structure*, pp. 131–160. Adherence to norm prescriptions in spite of the situational context may weaken role relationships and, in addition, impede the advance toward the goal. It is hard, of course, to know at what point excellence of effort stops and compulsive behavior begins.

[52] Goffman notes a form of tacit cooperation between the normals and the stigmatized which may be noted here: the normals tolerate the stigmatized because "the stigmatized will voluntarily refrain from pushing claims for acceptance much past the point normals find comfortable"; *op. cit.*, pp. 129–130.

[53] White's data showed that women lawyers see fewer clients than do male lawyers; "Women in the Law," p. 1093.

ual in nature. Younger women in professional life, however, seem to feel less reticent about joining colleagues for lunch. By bowing to pressure to make themselves unobtrusive or adopting the other mechanisms mentioned, women are accepting common definitions about the inappropriateness of their presence in the field in which they have chosen to work.

REACTIONS OF MEN

Men in the professions manifest similar discomfort in their interactions with female colleagues. They, too, overrespond. They feel uneasy and may try to compensate by being overly solicitous, congenial, courtly — or by demanding too little of the woman, or too much.

Many female medical students, responding to a questionnaire about their treatment in medical school, "described their teachers and colleagues as 'more courteous, more polite, concerned, respectful, patient, considerate, kinder, more gentle, easier, and less abusive.' Others felt they were singled out by instructors, that their errors were more easily noticed and remembered and that every failure on their part was ascribed to their sex." Women students in that same sample thought that their work "was not taken seriously by their instructors, that the faculty expectations of them were lower than for the men, and that a lower level of performance was accepted, stifling their incentive. On the other hand, a few felt that faculty expectations of them were higher than for the men, and that in fact they were required to work harder and to do better in order to be accepted as having done the same kind of job." [54]

It is clear that as far as standards of work are concerned, the woman professional's accomplishments are judged by a different set of standards than the man's. Minor accomplishments may be assessed as signs of remarkable and noteworthy capacities "in the circumstances." The woman benefiting from the

[54] Helen Glaser in a report to the Macy Conference on Women for Medicine, cited in Lopate, *op. cit.*, p. 81.

judgment may feel that she has been put down; the man making the assessment will probably feel only that he is trying to do the right thing.

On the other hand, some men make it clear that they expect the woman will not do well. Thus they expect more from the women who make it, assuming that the winners of the obstacle race must be clearly superior. Women in the better positions in professional life report that the men in their world expect them to be perfect, while their male peer is not placed on the same kind of rather precarious pedestal.

Status discrepancies make continuous role definition necessary during interactions that should be routine. As a result, all group members are sensitized to problems of ambiguity and are forced to form new ground rules (that is, establish norms) for each situation. When an inappropriate status of a status set is activated in a professional context, refocusing on the appropriate status must occur if the professional task is to be accomplished.

Situations Minimizing the Effects of Sex Status

There follow a number of circumstances in which the problems just identified do not come up, or in which they are minimal. Such situations make it possible for women to manage careers and to accomplish professional goals.

(*a*) The context is formal and the task is well-defined, so that no one is unsure about the norms governing the interaction, including authority patterns and division of labor. This is true of the classroom, the operating room, the courtroom.

(*b*) The standards of performance are clearly defined, can be measured, and lead to a specific result. For example, if a woman surgeon performs a delicate brain operation, her skill can be professionally evaluated. Others in the profession know what a successful operation is; her performance doing it is highly visible; the patient lives or dies, is mended or not.

(*c*) There are third parties who will support the professional interaction. The professor of medicine instructing a male and a female medical student in a laboratory will usually ensure that their relationship at work is task-directed.[55]

(*d*) The professional relationship is long-term and the participants establish a set of ground rules to govern behavior. For example, women lawyers who had worked in a firm for a number of years and who early set a precedent of paying their own way reported having no problems in suggesting lunching with colleagues.

(*e*) Women do not permit their own self-consciousness to cause them to overreact. Women who are professional but not especially formal or aggressive, who try to be gracious as women and not deny their sex, are said to be able to make the best impression on men and gain acceptance. Often sex status intrudes less when it is permitted expression in normal sex-role behavior. For example, women who work in tradition-bound law firms often find that male colleagues are used to treating women in a courtly manner and can work best with women who are comfortable with such treatment. Problems arise only where women demand they be treated "just like the men," causing their colleagues discomfort. Attempts to suppress sex-role behavior in such contexts only succeed in making it obtrusive.

(*f*) The firm or organization is of high rank and good reputation. Once a member of an elite group, a woman can expect more fair and open treatment on the average than in lower-ranking groups.[56] In low-ranking firms, where lawyers tend to be insecure about their ability and income potential, women get poor treatment. Not that better firms and institutions do not discriminate, but their treatment of employees tends generally to be considerate and more universalistic. Perhaps too, they can afford to "take chances" on a woman. Or, perhaps, their exclu-

[55] See William J. Goode, "Norm Commitment and Conformity to Role Status Obligations," *American Journal of Sociology* 66 (November 1960), 246–258.

[56] This is probably true only for professional organizations and not for business.

sionary devices are more subtle and therefore easier to ignore and more difficult to appraise.

(*g*) Ability can be clearly demonstrated. Performance counts in the legal profession, in medicine, and in science, and often is sufficient to reduce resistance to accepting of the woman who produces. Women in professional life counsel neophytes to make an effort to become experts in some specialty because their special talents will then be sought out regardless of their sex.

(*h*) Each party has a high stake in the task at hand and benefits from the professional status of the other. For example, an industrial engineer pays $50 an hour for the expert services of a female patent lawyer who, in turn, would like to keep him as a steady client.

(*i*) There is no clear status-set typing of an occupational role to complement the occupational status. New industries with an open personnel market often do not have traditions of exclusion or institutionalized mechanisms for supporting that exclusion.[57] Computer programming is an occupation which has not been sex-typed and very likely there is no agreement about what the appropriate sex status should be for a programmer.

Like others with status handicaps which do not conform to cultural preferences, women must learn the dynamics of dealing with inappropriate responses to their sex as well as learning the skills of their trade. Some women are protected by the social structure more than others; some have greater personal skill in handling people or ambiguities. The more a woman

---

[57] For example, there are proportionately more women engineers in newer fields such as interdisciplinary and chemical engineering; Aileen Cavanaugh, "Present Opportunities for Women in Professional Engineering," *Women in Professional Engineering*, p. 75. Women engineers and other professionals are often told to go West, for it is believed that they have more opportunities there than in the East, where attitudes are set concerning who may appropriately do what activity; Emma C. Barthm, "Opportunities for Women in Engineering," reprint of excerpts from an address delivered before the Educational Department, Congress of Women's Clubs, November 5, 1964, Pittsburgh, Pa.

can depend on the environment or filter out those responses to her sex status which intrude on the professional task, and the more she has perfected techniques for handing inappropriate responses, the more likely she is to continue at her work and proceed along a normal career sequence. American women can abandon their professional careers, no matter how high the investment in it or the amount of talent shown for it, with a high degree of cultural approval. The chances are that those women who enter professional life and remain in it are from environments that have minimized obstacles, or are women who have the good fortune to possess personalities that refuse to recognize the obstacles as more than the rough spots of any normal life. All other things being equal, fewer women than men are graduates of the school of hard knocks.

VI
PROFESSIONS IN A CHANGING WORLD: NEW CONTEXTS

ONLY unusual women have managed successfully to hold what American society considers high-level jobs along with the family roles historically assigned to women. They succeeded because they were able to mobilize intellect, physical energy, and administrative talent and because they lived in circumstances where the motivation to engage in responsible and creative work was developed, where the obstacles were few, and where the networks of family, friends, and colleagues were supportive.

Not all of these factors are necessarily involved in the basic equation of women's success, but each instance encountered in the course of this work has been marked by something special. Some women with modest talents have been able to develop themselves fully because ambitious parents directed them into careers. Others with great drive and ability have had to struggle against the objections of family to enter professional work. Some women never face discrimination; others find ways to surmount it. But as we have seen, all have found that it is difficult for women to exercise their right to share in the meaningful work of society.

Among those who somehow manage to balance the responsibilities of home and careers, the small percentage of women who find their way into the male-dominated professions experience obstacles to full membership and to the accomplishment of their tasks. Above everything else stands the fact that they are women and that a large proportion of American men and women think that they ought not, or cannot, engage in professional activity. This book has examined mechanisms used by professional women and by their colleagues to adjust to the "disturbances" caused by those women entering professional life, as well as the mechanisms they use to meet their responsibilities as wives and mothers. Most of these solutions are idiosyncratic; none are institutionalized.

We do, however, live in an era marked by rapid social changes, and many of these changes should affect the relationships and images that limit or enhance women's horizons. Although there seems to be no evidence of radical change in the recruitment and involvement of women in the professions, or any appreciable change in family institutions that might permit better integration of work in women's lives, there have been wider societal changes that may contribute to the greater participation of women and lighten the burdens assumed by today's professional women.

The cumulative effect of these changes should lead to the opening of opportunities at all stages of career development, but particularly at the point of entry into the professions, where opposition to women's participation has been greatest. Their direction will depend on the strength and durability of several trends.

First, there is a growing participation in work by women in other countries. Although the United States was the first nation to grant women social and legal equality, women have made striking strides toward positions of power, prestige, and deci-

TABLE II

Female Workers in Selected Occupations and Professions
(U.S., 1870–1960)

Occupation	1870	1880	1890	1900	1910	1920	1930	1940	1950[h]	1960[h]
Accountants and auditors									56,884	80,483
College presidents, professors, instructors[a]					2,928	9,974	19,930	20,124	29,267	39,168
Engineers,										
Electrical					6	12	62	224	1,237	1,561
Civil and surveyors				51	5	18	29	332	1,932[g]	700[g]
Other								188	970	726
Mechanical			21	30		11		228	576	557
Industrial							18	74	450	2,266
Sales										101
Chemical				3			4	59	629	542
Aeronautical									331	778
Mining and metallurgical								74	350	300
Editors and reporters	43	357	1,101	2,719	5,184	7,105	14,786	15,890	28,595	
Lawyers and judges					558	1,738	3,385	4,447	6,348	7,543
Natural scientists[b]		49	40	253	591	1,748	1,963	1,734	13,654	15,052
Nurses,[c]										
Professional	1,154	1,464	4,206	11,046	76,508	143,664	228,737	362,897	395,638	577,038
Student professional									75,344	56,745

Occupation	1870	1880	1890	1900	1910	1920	1930	1940	1950[h]	1960[h]
Physicians and surgeons[d]	554	2,432	4,557	7,387	9,015	7,219	6,825	7,708	11,823	15,672
Social scientists									11,667	14,375
Librarians[e]	43	323	2,752	3,184	5,771	13,367	26,785	39,546	49,356	72,357
Teachers[f]	84,585	153,372	244,467	325,485	476,864	635,207	853,976	802,264	844,121	1,205,681
Midwives					6,208	4,773	3,566			
Social and welfare workers, religious workers	65	157	1,086	3,204	9,308	28,109	47,069	48,369	60,291	78,017

Sources: U.S. Bureau of the Census, 1960. Subject Reports. *Occupational Characteristics*, Final Report PC(2)–7A, 1963, Table 21; and *Statistical Abstract of the U.S.* (1925), Table 328.

Data 1870–1940: J. M. Hooks, *Women's Occupations Through Seven Decades*, Women's Bureau, Dept. of Labor (Washington, D.C.: U.S. Government Printing Office, 1947).

Data for 1950: U.S. Bureau of the Census, Census of Population, 1950. Vol. II, *Characteristics of the Population*, Part I, U.S. Summary, Table 124, pp. 1–261.

1960 figures: U.S. Bureau of the Census, Census of Population, 1960. Subject Reports. *Occupational Characteristics*, Final Report PC(2)–7A, 1963, Table 21, p. 277.

[a] Combined with teachers until 1910.

[b] Chemist only 1880–1940.

[c] Combined until 1950.

[d] 1870–1900 includes chiropracters and other health workers.

[e] 1870–1900 includes authors.

[f] 1870–1900 with college presidents and professors.

[g] 1950, 1960, Civil Engineers, surveyors *excluded*. Their numbers are 996 in 1950, 1,690 in 1960.

[h] 1950, 1960, *employed* persons, *not* experienced civilian labor force.

sion in other countries. In addition, the accelerated rate at which great numbers of women in underdeveloped countries have taken their place in the modern world is bound to reinforce pressure for further improvement in the position of women in the great industrial societies, including of course the United States. Indian women, Vietnamese women, Chinese women, all have won more concessions to equality with men in the past decade or two than in the preceding thousand years. Although there is no great competition between nations to advance the position of women, no nation can risk totally ignoring the social advances evident in other countries. In the past few years the United States has taken steps to reduce inequities through the President's Commission on the Status of Women and other agencies, such as the Equal Employment Opportunities Commission.

Second, although the proportion of women in the male-dominated professions has not dramatically increased (and in some cases has decreased), there has been an increase in absolute numbers of women in professional life.[1] This means that women engaged in these pursuits are more visible, and it no longer seems peculiar or impossible for them to be part of any profession. Table 11 indicates the considerable increases of numbers of women in certain occupations since the turn of the century.

Third, the scope of professional activity has expanded. There is increasingly an urgent need for trained personnel. Government work, civil rights programs such as the N.A.A.C.P. and N.A.A.C.P. Legal Defense and Education Fund antipoverty programs funded by the Office of Economic Opportunity,[2] community health programs, new areas of technology (information retrieval and computer processing, for example), all mean more jobs, jobs which fall outside the traditional occupations and do not carry the traditional prejudices. At the very

---

[1] Merton has commented on the consequences of absolute and relative size for group interaction; *Social Theory and Social Structure*, pp. 175, 313, 411.

[2] The Office of Economic Opportunity has created 1,200 staff jobs since it started offering legal services to the poor in 1965. See "The 'New Law' *vs.* Tradition," *Newsweek* (June 19, 1967), p. 104.

least, the emergence of these fields means more competition for talent. Bright young men have their choice of many more attractive positions than ever before, creating a shortage of desirable personnel in the older elite fields.[3] The gatekeepers of the traditional occupations will be forced to admit many who qualify professionally but do not conform to the old social specifications. Talented women provide a ready source of able personnel waiting to be tapped.

Fourth, schools are recruiting from a wider social base. This means not only that more young people have a chance for professional training, but that the experience of studying with fellow students from varied backgrounds will minimize any tendency of future professionals to expect their colleagues to fit the old stereotypes. Further, young men now are apparently more at ease working with educated women, especially those educated at the elite institutions, which are fast becoming coeducational. Once strictly segregated, Ivy League schools such as Harvard now permit "sister" colleges to participate fully in their educational programs. Radcliffe College will soon merge with Harvard. Yale recently announced that five hundred young women will be enrolled as full-time students as the first step toward a coeducational student body, and Princeton is in the process of becoming decloistered. Young men will be less resistant to working with women if they have had the experience of studying with them as classmates in college and in professional training.[4] There is some evidence that the younger men taking command in the decision-making centers are more receptive to employing women than were their predecessors.

[3] See Erwin O. Smigel, *The Wall Street Lawyer*, p. 64, for an account of changing recruitment policies in the old and large New York City law firms.

[4] *The American Soldier* studies indicated that when those of unequal status found themselves working together, they changed their former attitudes about each other and became accepting. Situations may not only structure behavior, but may change specific attitudes in the process. The studies indicated that white soldiers' attitudes toward Negroes as fighting men changed when they were battle companions, although the acceptance was situation-specific and did not extend to acceptance of them as social companions; Stouffer *et. al., The American Soldier: Studies in Social Psychology in World War II*, Vol. I. Thus, the altering of structure may do part of the job; ease in informal interaction in the professional context would probably come later.

Fifth, the "halo effect" generally results when barriers break down in one institution. Once opportunities open for women in institutions of higher learning, particularly in those which offer professional training, opportunities may be expected to open in the working institutions. Many major Boston law firms that were firmly resistant even to interviewing women for law positions did hire a few when the Harvard Law School finally decided to admit them in 1950. Once a breach is found in the barriers of tradition, it may be expected that it will be expanded to become a passageway.

Finally, recent ideological changes have affected women as well as men. Surveys show that college-educated women now are more likely to use their training than was true previously. Perhaps this change in the behavior and expectations of women may create a greater drive for recognition and success.

Although women's special problems have not been publicized to the same extent as those of other disadvantaged groups, women's position in the occupations may be enhanced by the pressures growing throughout society to grant equal opportunity to all. It is difficult to predict whether the trends toward equality will be stronger than the forces peculiarly inhibiting women in their choice and opportunity of working equally with men at all levels of the occupational hierarchy. Only with a significant increase in their numbers in the male-dominated occupations and with a restructuring of expectations about women's place in society will women be able to work and compete with men freely at all levels of performance.

BIBLIOGRAPHY

American Medical Women's Association, Research Comm. 1966 Report (unpublished).

American Science Manpower. National Science Foundation, NSF 66–29. Washington, D.C.: U.S. Government Printing Office, 1964.

American Women 1963–1968: Report of the Interdepartmental Committee on the Status of Women. Washington, D.C.: U.S. Government Printing Office, 1968.

Angel, Jurenal Londen. *Careers for Women in the Legal Profession.* New York: New York World Trade Academy Press, 1961.

Armstrong, Barbara. "2,997 Women Practice Law in U.S., Still Find Going Tough, Survey Shows." *Harvard Law School Record* 13 (December 6, 1951), 1 ff.

Bailyn, Lotte. "Notes on the Role of Choice in the Psychology of Professional Women." *Daedalus* 93 (Spring 1964), 700–710.

Barber, Bernard. "Resistance by Scientists to Scientific Discovery," 539–536. In B. Barber and W. Hirsh (eds.). *The Sociology of Science.* New York: The Free Press of Glencoe, 1962.

Barker, Roger G. "The Social Psychology of Physical Disability." *Journal of Social Issues* 4 (Fall 1968), 28–54.

Bayer, Alan E., and Helen S. Astin. "Sex Differences in Academic Rank and Salary Among Science Doctorates in Teaching." *Journal of Human Resources* 3 (Spring 1968), 191–200.

Beck, E. Wilbur. "The Female Clergy: A Case of Professional Marginality." *American Journal of Sociology* 72 (March 1967), 531–539.

Becker, Howard, and James Carper. "Development of Identification with an Occupation." *American Journal of Sociology* 61 (January 1956), 289–298.

Becker, Howard, and Anselm Strauss. "Careers, Personality, and Adult Socialization." *American Journal of Sociology* 62 (November 1956), 253–263.

Bernard, Jessie. *Academic Women.* University Park, Pa.: The Pennsylvania State University Press, 1964.

———. "The Status of Women in Modern Patterns of Culture." *Annals of the American Academy of Political and Social Science* 375 (January 1968), 3–14.

Bettelheim, Bruno. "Growing Up Female." *Harper's* (October 1962), pp. 120–123.

Blau, Peter, John W. Gustad, Richard Jessor, Herbert S. Parnes, and Richard C. Wilcock. "Occupational Choice: A Conceptual Framework." *Industrial and Labor Relations Review* 9 (July 1956), 531–543.

Blaustein, Albert P., and Howard S. Kaplan. "America's Women Lawyers: The 1949 'Lawyer-Count.'" *Women Lawyers' Journal* 37, No. 2 (1951), 18–20.

Boring, Edwin. "The Woman Problem." *American Psychologist* (December 6, 1951), pp. 679–682.

Bronfenbrenner, Urie. "Socialization and Social Class Through Time and Space," pp. 400–425. In Eleanor E. Maccoby, Theodore M. Newcomb, Eugene L. Harley. *Readings in Social Psychology*. New York: Holt, Rinehart and Winston, Inc., 1958, Third Edition.

Brown, Donald. "Some Education Patterns." *Journal of Social Issues*, 1956, 12 (4), 44–60.

Bryan, Alice I., and Edwin G. Boring. "Women in American Psychology: Factors Affecting Their Professional Careers." *American Psychologist* 2 (January 1947), 3–20.

Bunting, Mary I. "A Huge Waste: Education Womanpower." *New York Times Magazine* (May 7, 1961), p. 23.

———. "Our Greatest Waste of Talent Is Women." *Life* (January 13, 1961), pp. 63–64.

Carlin, Jerome. *Lawyers on Their Own*. New Brunswick, N.J.: Rutgers University Press, 1962.

———. *Lawyers' Ethics*. New York: Russell Sage Foundation, 1966.

Carper, James W. "The Development of Identification with an Occupation." *American Journal of Sociology* 61 (January 1956), 296.

Castle, Cora. *A Statistical Study of Eminent Women*. New York: Reprinted from the *Archives of Psychology*, No. 27; Ph.D. dissertation, Columbia University, August 1913.

Caute, David. "Crisis in All Souls." *Encounter* 26 (1966), 3–15.

Cavanaugh, Aileen. "Present Opportunities for Women in Professional Engineering." *Women in Professional Engineering*. New York: Society of Women Engineers, 1962.

Cole, Steven, and Jonathan R. Cole. "Visibility and the Structural Bases of Awareness of Scientific Research." *American Sociological Review* 33 (June 1968), 397–413.

Collier, Virginia MacMakin. *Marriage and Careers: A Study of One Hundred Women Who Are Wives, Mothers, Homemakers and Professional Women*. New York: The Channel Bookshop, 1926.

David, Opal D. (ed.) *The Education of Women: Signs for the Future*. Washington, D.C.: American Council on Education, 1959.

Davis, Fred, and Virginia L. Oleson. "Initiation into a Woman's Profession: Identity Problems in the Status Transition of Coed to Student Nurse." *Sociometry* 26 (March 1963), 89–101.

Davis, James. *Great Aspirations*. Chicago: Aldine Publishing Company, 1964.

Davis, Kingsley. "The Sociology of Parent-Youth Conflict." *American Sociological Review* 4 (August 1940), 423–435.

Degler, Carl N. "Revolution Without Ideology: The Changing Place of Women in America." *Daedalus* (Spring 1964), 653–670.

Diamond, M. C. "Women in Modern Science." *Journal of the American Medical Women's Association* 18 (November 1963), 891–896.

Dodge, Norton T. *Women in the Soviet Economy*. Baltimore: Johns Hopkins Press, 1966.

Dunham, Ralph E., Patricia D. Wright, and Marjorie O. Chandler. *Higher Colleges*. U.S. Office of Education. Washington, D.C.: U.S. Government Printing Office, 1966.

————. Patricia D. Wright, and Marjorie O. Chandler. "Teaching Faculty in Universities and Four-Year Colleges." U.S. Office of Education. Washington, D.C.: U.S. Government Printing Office, 1966.

"Education in Britain." British Information Service (January 1964).

Epstein, Cynthia Fuchs. "Women and Professional Careers: The Case of the Woman Lawyer." Unpublished Ph.D. dissertation, Columbia University, 1968.

Etzioni, Amitai. *A Comparative Analysis of Complex Organizations*. New York: The Free Press of Glencoe, 1961.

Farber, Seymour M., and Roger H. L. Wilson (eds.). *The Potential of Women*. New York: McGraw-Hill Paperbacks, 1963.

Fava, Sylvia. "The Status of Women in Professional Sociology." *American Sociological Review* 25 (1960), 271–272.

Franz, Nellie Alden. *English Women Enter the Professions*. Cincinnati, Ohio: Privately printed by Columbia University Press, 1965.

Friedan, Betty. *The Feminine Mystique*. New York: W. W. Norton and Co., 1963.

Friedman, Mervin. "The Passage Through College." *Journal of Social Issues* 12, No. 4 (1956), 13–28.

Gans, Herbert. *The Urban Villagers*. New York: The Free Press of Glencoe, 1962.

Geiger, H. Kent. *The Family in Soviet Russia*. Cambridge, Mass.: Harvard University Press, 1968.

Ginder, Charles. "The Factor of Sex in Office Employment." *Office Executive* (February 1961), p. 10.

Ginzberg, Eli. *Occupational Choice*. New York: Columbia University Press, 1951.

Gittelson, Natalie. "Her Excellency, the Prime Minister." *Harper's Bazaar* (June 1966), pp. 100 ff.

Goffman, Erving. *Encounters*. Indianapolis: Bobbs-Merrill Co., 1961.

Goffman, Erving. *Stigma: Notes on the Management of Spoiled Identity.*
Englewood Cliffs, N.J.: Prentice-Hall, 1963.
Goode, William J. "Community Within a Community: The Professions."
American Sociological Review 22 (1957), 195–200.
———. *The Family.* Englewood Cliffs, N.J.: Prentice-Hall, 1964.
———. "Norm Commitment and Conformity to Role Statcs Obligations."
American Journal of Sociology 66 (November 1960), 246–258.
———. "The Protection of the Inept." *American Sociological Review* 32
(1967), 5–18.
———. "The Theoretical Importance of Love." *American Sociological
Review* 24 (1959), 38–47.
———. "A Theory of Role Strain." *American Sociological Review* 25
(August 1960), 483–496.
———. *Women in Divorce.* New York: The Free Press of Glencoe, 1956;
published under this title as a Free Press Paperback.
———. *World Revolution and Family Patterns.* New York: The Free
Press of Glencoe, 1963.
Griffin, Verna Elizabeth. *Employment Opportunities for Women in Legal
Work.* U.S. Department of Labor, Washington, D.C.: U.S. Govern-
ment Printing Office, 1958.
Guilbert, Madeleine. *Les Fonctions des femmes dans l'industrie.* Paris:
Mouton & Cie., 1966.
Hacker, Helen. "A Functional Approach to the Gainful Employment of
Married Women." Unpublished Ph.D. dissertation, Columbia Uni-
versity, 1961.
———. "Women as a Minority Group." *Social Forces* 30 (October 1951),
60–69.
Hall, Edward T. *The Silent Language.* New York: Premier Books, 1963.
Handbook of Women Workers, 1962. U.S. Department of Labor, Wom-
en's Bureau Bulletin 285. Washington, D.C.: U.S. Government Printing
Office, 1963.
Handbook of Women Workers, 1965. U.S. Department of Labor, Wom-
en's Bureau Bulletin 290. Washington, D.C.: U.S. Government Printing
Office, 1966.
Havemann, E., and P. West. *They Went to College: The College Graduate
in America Today.* New York: Harcourt, Brace and Co., 1952.
Havighurst, Robert J. *Growing up in River City.* New York: John Wiley
and Sons, 1962.
Hawkes, Anna L. Rose. "Factors Affecting College Attendance." In
Opal D. David (ed.). *The Education of Women: Signs for the Future.*
Washington, D.C.: American Council on Education, 1959.
Helfrich, Margaret. "The Generalized Role of the Executive's Wife."
Marriage and Family Living 23–24 (1961), 384–387.
Hooks, Janet. *Women's Occupations Through Seven Decades (1870–
1940).* U.S. Department of Labor, Women's Bureau Bulletin 218.

Washington, D.C.: U.S. Government Printing Office, 1947.
Hughes, Everett C. "Dilemmas and Contradiction of Status." *American Journal of Sociology* 50 (1945), 353–359.
Hunt, Morton H. "The Direction of Feminine Evolution," pp. 255–271. In Seymour M. Farber and Roger H. L. Wilson (eds.). *The Potential of Women.* New York: McGraw-Hill Paperbacks, 1963.
Huseboe, Doris L. "An Examination of Women in the Law Profession." Unpublished paper, Indiana University, 1959.
Inkeles, Alex. "Social Change and Social Character: The Role of Parental Mediation." *Journal of Social Issues* 11, No. 2 (1955), 12–22.
Jeffers, William N. "How the Specialties Compare Financially." *Medical Economics* 44 (February 6, 1967), 71.
Jeffreys, Margot, and Patricia M. Elliott. *Women in Medicine: The Results of an Inquiry Conducted by the Medical Practitioners' Union in 1962–63.* London: Office of Health Economics, 1966.
Johnson, Davis G. "The Study of Applicants, 1964–1965." *Journal of Medical Education* 40, No. 11 (1965), 1026–1027.
Kammeyer, Kenneth. "Birth Order and the Feminine Sex Role Among College Women." *American Sociological Review* 31 (1966), 508–515.
Komarovsky, Mirra. "The Functional Analysis of Sex Roles." *American Sociological Review* 15 (1950), 508–516; reprinted in Marvin Sussman (ed.), *Sourcebook on Marriage and the Family.* Boston: Houghton Mifflin Co., Third Edition, 1968, 258–266.
———. "Cultural Contradictions and Sex Roles." *American Journal of Sociology* 52 (November 1946), 184–189.
———. *Women in the Modern World: Their Education and Their Dilemmas.* Boston: Houghton Mifflin Co., 1953.
Kosa, John, and Robert E. Coker, Jr. "The Female Physician in Public Health: Conflict and Reconciliation of the Professional and Sex Roles." *Sociology and Social Research* 49 (April 1965), 295.
Kucera, Daniel J. "Women Unwanted." *Harvard Law Review* 37 (December 12, 1963), 1 ff.
Ladinsky, Jack. "Careers of Lawyers, Law Practice, and Legal Institutions." *American Sociological Review* 28 (1963), 47–54.
Lavin, David E. *The Prediction of Academic Performance.* New York: Russell Sage Foundation, 1965.
Lynd, Robert. *Knowledge for What: The Place of Social Sciences in American Culture.* New York: Grove Press, 1964.
Lipset, Seymour Martin. *The First New Nation.* New York: Basic Books 1963.
Lopate, Carole. *Women in Medicine.* Baltimore: Johns Hopkins Press, 1968.
Low, Seth, and Pearl G. Spindler. *Child Care Arrangements of Working Mothers in the United States.* Washington, D.C.: U.S. Government Printing Office, Children's Bureau Publication 461, 1968.

McClelland, David. *The Achieving Society.* New York: D. Van Nostrand Co., 1961.

McGrew, Elizabeth, M.D., Barbara Christine, M.D., Charlotte Kerr, M.D., Miss Marguerite Gilmore, Rose Lee Nemir M.D. "Medical Womenpower: Can It Be Used More Effectively?" *Journal of the American Medical Women's Association* 17 (December 1962), 973–985.

Matthews, Esther. "The Marriage-Career Conflict in the Career Development of Girls and Young Women." Unpublished Ph.D. dissertation, Harvard University, 1960.

Maccoby, Eleanor (ed.). *The Development of Sex Differences.* Stanford, Calif.: Stanford University Press, 1966.

Mace, David, and Vera Mace. *The Soviet Family.* New York: Doubleday, Dolphin Books, 1964.

Mattfeld, Jacquelyn A., and Carol G. Van Aken (eds.). *Women and the Scientific Professions.* Cambridge, Mass.: The M.I.T. Press, 1965.

Mead, Margaret (ed.). *Anthropologist at Work: The Writings of Ruth Benedict.* Boston: Houghton Mifflin Co., 1959.

———. *Sex and Temperament in Three Primitive Societies.* New York: William Morrow and Co., 1935.

——— and Frances Balgley Kaplan (eds.). *American Women: Report of the President's Commission on the Status of Women and Other Publications of the Commission.* New York: Charles Scribner's Sons, 1965.

Merton, Robert K. "The Role Set: Problems in Sociological Theory." *British Journal of Sociology* 8 (June 1957), 106–120.

———. *Social Theory and Social Structure.* Revised edition. Glencoe, Ill.: The Free Press, 1957.

——— and Elinor Barber. "Sociological Ambivalence," pp. 91–120. In Edward A. Tiryakian (ed.). *Sociological Theory, Values and Sociological Change.* New York: The Free Press of Glencoe, 1963.

———. *Some Thoughts on the Professions in American Society.* Providence, R.I.: Brown University papers, No. 37, 1960.

Merton, Robert K., George Reader, and Patricia Kendall (eds.). *The Student Physician.* Cambridge, Mass.: Harvard University Press, 1957.

Merton, Robert K., Samuel Bloom, and Natalie Rogoff. "Studies in the Sociology of Medical Education." *Journal of Medical Education* 31 (August 1956), 552–565.

Mitchell, Mildred B. "Status of Women in the American Psychological Association." *American Psychologist* 6 (1951), 193–201.

National Research Council. *Doctorate Production in U.S. Universities, 1920–1962.* Washington, D.C.: National Academy of Sciences, 1963.

Newcomer, Mabel. *A Century of Higher Education for Women.* New York: Harper and Brothers, 1959.

"The 'New Law' *vs.* Tradition." *Newsweek* (June 19, 1967), p. 104.

O'Gorman, Hubert J. *Lawyers and Matrimonial Cases.* New York: The Free Press of Glencoe, 1963.

Packard, Vance. *The Sexual Wilderness: The Contemporary Upheaval in Male-Female Relationships.* New York: David McKay Co., 1968.

Parrish, John B. "Professional Womanpower as a National Resource." *Quarterly Review of Education and Business* (February 1961), pp. 54–63.

Parsons, Talcott. "Age and Sex in the Social Structure of the United States." *Essays in Sociological Theory.* Rev. ed. Glencoe, Ill.: The Free Press, 1954.

Petersen, Esther. "Working Women." *Daedalus* 93 (Spring 1964), pp. 671–699.

"Profile of the Woman Engineer." Statistics Committee. New York: Society of Women Engineers, 1963.

Reiss, Ira L. *Social Context of Premarital Sexual Permissiveness.* New York: Holt, Rinehart, and Winston, 1967.

Report of the Task Force on Labor Standards to the Citizens' Advisory Council on the Status of Women, April 1968. Washington, D.C.: Citizens' Advisory Council on the Status of Women. Washington, D.C.: U.S. Government Printing Office, 1968.

Ridley, Jeanne Clare. "Demographic Change and the Roles and Status of Women." *Annals of the American Academy of Political and Social Science* 375 (January 1968), 15–25.

Roper, Elmo. "Women in America." Fortune Survey, Part II. *Fortune* (September 1946), pp. 5–6.

Rose, Arnold. "The Adequacy of Women's Expectations for Adult Roles." *Social Forces* 30, No. 6 (October 1951), 69–77.

Rosenlund, Mary Loretta, and Frank A. Oski, M.D. "Women in Medicine." *Annals of Internal Medicine* 66 (1967), 1008–1012.

Rosenmayr, Leopold. "The Austrian Women." *International Social Science Journal* 14, No. 1 (1962), 157–165.

Ross, Dorothy Robinson. "The Story of the Top 1 Percent of the Women at Michigan State University." East Lansing, Mich.: Counseling Center, Michigan State University, 1963. Mimeographed.

Rossi, Alice S. "Barriers to the Career Choice of Engineering, Medicine or Science Among American Women," pp. 51–127. In Jacquelyn A. Mattfeld and Carol G. Van Aken (eds.). *Women and the Scientific Professions.* Cambridge, Mass.: The M.I.T. Press, 1965.

———. "Equality Between the Sexes: An Immodest Proposal." *Daedalus* 93 (Spring 1964), 607–652.

———. "A Good Woman Is Hard to Find." *Transaction* 2, No. 1 (November–December 1964), 20–23.

———. "Women in Science: Why so Few?" *Science* 148, No. 3674 (May 28, 1965), 1196–1202.

Simon, Rita James, Shirley Merritt Clark, and Kathleen Galway. "The Woman Ph.D." *Social Problems* 15 (Fall 1967), 221–236.

Smigel, Erwin. *The Wall Street Lawyer.* New York: The Free Press of Glencoe, 1964.

Stafford, Rita Lynne. "An Analysis of Consciously Recalled Professional Involvement for American Women in New York State." Unpublished Ph.D. dissertation, New York University, 1966.

Stouffer, Samuel A., Edward Suchman, Leland C. De Vinney, Shirley A. Star, and Robin M. Williams, Jr. *The American Soldier: Studies in Social Psychology in World War II.* Princeton, N.J.: Princeton University Press, 1949.

Study of Employment of Women in the Federal Government, 1967. U.S. Civil Service Commission Statistics Section. Washington, D.C.: U.S. Government Printing Office, June 1968, p. 3.

Smuts, Robert W. *Women and Work in America.* New York: Columbia University Press, 1959.

Super, Donald. *Psychology of Careers.* New York: Harper and Brothers, 1957.

Sutheim, Susan. "Women Shake Up SDS Session." *National Guardian* (June 22, 1968), p. 6.

Sutherland, Robert. "Some Basic Facts." In Opal D. David, ed. *The Education of Women: Signs for Future.* Washington, D.C.: American Council on Education, 1959.

Tavistock Institute. *Women and Top Jobs: An Interim Report.* London: Political and Economic Planning, 1967.

Thielens, Wagner, Jr. "The Socialization of Law Students: A Case Study in Three Parts." Unpublished Ph.D. dissertation, Columbia University, 1965.

Tomasson, Richard F. "The Swedes Do It Better." *Harper's* (October 1962), pp. 178–180.

Turner, Marjorie B. *Women and Work.* Los Angeles: Institute of Industrial Relations, University of California, 1964.

U.S. Department of Labor. *Changes in Women's Occupations, 1940–50.* Women's Bureau Bulletin 253. Washington, D.C.: U.S. Government Printing Office, 1954.

Warkov, Seymour, and Joseph Zelan. *Lawyers in the Making.* Chicago: Aldine Publishing Co., 1965.

"What Educated Women Want." *Newsweek* (June 13, 1966), pp. 68–75.

White, James J. "Women in the Law." *Michigan Law Review* 65 (April 1967), 1051–1122.

Whiteside, Elena. "For Soviet Women: A Thirteen-Hour Day." *New York Times Magazine* (November 17, 1963), pp. 28 ff.

Who's Who of American Women. Fourth Eition (1966–67). Chicago: The A. N. Marquis Co., 1966. Also Fifth Edition (1968–69).

Whyte, William F. "The Wife Problem." *Life* (January 7, 1952), pp. 32–48. Reprinted in Winch, McGinnis, and Barringer.

Wilensky, Harold. "The Professionalization of Everyone?" *American Journal of Sociology* 70 (1964), 137–158.

Williams, Josephine J. "Patients and Prejudice: Lay Attitudes Toward

Women Physicians." *American Journal of Sociology* 51 (1946), 283–287.

———. "The Professional Status of Women in Medicine." Unpublished Ph.D. dissertation, University of Chicago, 1949.

———. "The Woman Physician's Dilemma." *Journal of Social Issues* 6 (1950), 38–44.

Winick, Charles. *The New People: Desexualization in American Life* New York: Pegasus, 1968.

Winch, Robert F., Robert McGinnis, and Herbert R. Baringer (eds.) *Selected Studies in Marriage and Family.* New York: Holt, Rinehart, and Winston, 1962.

Young, Nancy. "Alumnae." *Harvard Law School Bulletin* (December 1956), pp. 12–13 *ff.*

Yudkin, Simon, and Anthea Holme. *Working Mothers and Their Children.* London: Michael Joseph and Co., 1963.

Zapoleon, Marguerite. "College Women and Employment," pp. 56–63. In Opal D. David (ed.). *The Education of Women: Signs for the Future.* Washington, D.C.: American Council on Education, 1959.

Zazewski, Henry C. *Child Care Arrangements of Full-Time Working Mothers.* Washington, D.C.; U.S. Department of Health Education and Welfare, Children's Bureau Publication 378, 1959.

Zborowski, Mark, and Elizabeth Herzog. *Life Is with People.* New York: Schocken Books, 1952.

Zinberg, Norman. "Psychiatry: A Professional Dilemma." *Daedalus* 92 (1963), 808–823.

Zuckerman, Harriet. "Nobel Laureates in Science: Patterns of Productivity, Collaboration, and Authorship." *American Sociological Review* 32 (1967), 393.

INDEX

Dr. Epstein is Assistant Professor of Sociology, Queens College of the City University of New York, a project director at the Bureau of Applied Social Research, Columbia University, and an associate of the Center for Policy Research.

DATE DUE

NOV 16 '71	FEB 26 '74	NOV 20 '84	
E H		NOV 5 '84	
FEB 1 '72	MAY 5 '74	DEC 0 7 1995	
APR 9 '72	OCT 28 '75	DEC 2 0 1995	
	NOV 11 '75		
MAY 15 '73	NOV 5 '77		
E H	NOV 10 '77		
SEP 17 '73	FEB 2 0 '79		
E H			
SEP 27 '73	MAR 7 '79		
E H	OCT 3 0 '79		
OCT 14 '73	OCT 24 '79		
E H	FEB 24 '81		
OCT 21 '73	FEB 25 '81		
E H	MAY 12 '81		
OCT 29 '73	MAY 12 '81		
E H	MAY 26 '81		
NOV 18 '73	MAY 19 '81		
GAYLORD			PRINTED IN U.S.A.